Ted Bunay

The Account of a Sociopathic Serial Killer

(Inside the Mind of of America's Most Glorified Serial Killer)

Hunter Parsons

Published By **Darby Connor**

Hunter Parsons

Ted Bundy: The Account of a Sociopathic Serial Killer (Inside the Mind of of America's Most Glorified Serial Killer)

ISBN 978-1-998038-64-0

Legal & Disclaimer

The information contained in this book is not designed to replace or take the place of any form of medicine or professional medical advice. The information in this book has been provided for educational & entertainment purposes only.

The information contained in this book has been compiled from sources deemed reliable, and it is accurate to the best of the Author's knowledge; however, the Author cannot guarantee its accuracy and validity and cannot be held liable for any errors or omissions. Changes are periodically made to this book. You must consult your doctor or get professional medical advice before using any of the suggested remedies, techniques, or information in this book.

Table Of Contents

Chapter 1: The First Time

"No person knows the exact date or the location Theodore "Ted" Bundy killed for first time. It may have occurred in his teens or just entering his 20s or the 1960s. The location could have been Washington State, where he lived for a long time, or perhaps on the East Coast, where he was born and was young man and also had connections to his family. However, we know for certain that in 1974, Ted Bundy's infamous rampage of murder and terror was in full swing. In Washington State, young, attractive female college students began disappearing. Police from the local area investigated and the first clues started to appear. People who witnessed the scene pointed to an Volkswagen Beetle and a young man who was on crutches, or an arm wrapped in a sling. Bundy relocated from Salt Lake City to Salt Lake City that summer as the killings took place across Utah, Idaho, and Colorado. The police in August of 1975 were able to arrest Bundy for first time, after pulling the vehicle over in his Volkswagen and spotting suspicious objects, including ropes, handcuffs and a ski mask that investigators later identified with missing women. The following February year, Bundy was convicted guilty of abducting and assaulting an Utah teenager who was able to elude him being imprisoned for at least 15 years. In the meantime, investigators from various states had been putting the series of murders. In the year 1976 Bundy was charged with murdering the nursing student who was on vacation and then he was arrested at Aspen, Colorado in June 1977 to appear before a preliminari hearing. In one instance, left on his own, Bundy let himself out through a window on the second floor then jogged back down Main Street, and disappeared." - - The FBI report of the Bundy case

There is no way to tell if anyone was born as to be a serial murderer. Indeed, the concept that a toddler might already be a victim in his heart the need for killing is incompatible with our human nature. But, there were alarms early on in Cowell's life. Theodore Robert Cowell, who was born on the 2nd of November 1946 in The Elizabeth Lund Home for Unwed mothers located in Burlington, Vermont. Louise Cowell's mother was the one who gave birth to him. Louise identified a person named Lloyd Marshall as his father however, she later claimed that his actual father was a different. Following her recovery from birth, her parents, Samuel and Eleanor took their son and daughter back home to

Philadelphia and gave the child their own during the initial 3 years of his existence. The young Ted was awed by Samuel, whom he believed be his father. However, Samuel himself was believed to have been brutal and perhaps even schizophrenia-prone individual who was known for abusing individuals and animals alike. Eleanor was also exhibiting signs of mental illness such as anxiety, depression, and agoraphobia. She received regular electroconvulsive therapy.

In tragically for the Cowell family and many others, Ted was believed to be a heir of every one of the signs for his grandparents' ailments, yet no of the social constraints that helped keep the older Cowell's under control. His aunt Julia told him a tale that she awoke to find that the 3-year-old boy was encircling her mattress with knives. Of course, the question what is the truth about whether or not this incident actually was as sinister in the moment as it was later revealed in the past as toddlers are known to have a tendency to engage in all sorts of strange actions without turning into serial murderers.

After this event, Louise suddenly decided to bring her son with her and relocate across the nation and relocate to Tacoma, Washington. In Tacoma, she was known as Louise Nelson, lived with her siblings, Alan as well as Jane Scott, and attended the First Methodist Church. At one evening of their singles when she came across Johnny Bundy, a cook in the hospital nearby. When they got married on the same day in 1952 Bundy took on the name Ted and changed his name to. In the now-famous appearance on James Dobson, Bundy recalled, "I grew up in the most wonderful house with two loving and committed parents. As one of five siblings and brothers. The home was where I as kids were the center of my parents' lives. Our church attendance was regular. We had two Christian parents. They didn't drink, didn't smoke, there wasn't any gambling and there was never physical violence or fights in the house. It's not like I'm saying ...'Leave the responsibility for Beaver '...but this was certainly a solid, fine Christian family home. It is my hope that anyone will use the easy route out or charge or blame my family members for contributing to this, because I'm sure the truth, and am trying to explain truthfully as I understand the circumstances of what transpired."

Dobson

One of the more controversial sections of the interview Bundy was able to talk about the circumstances that he encountered while he was still an infant. "But in my early years as a teenager (and I'm talking about boys aged twelve or thirteen, certainly) I was exposed in the outside of my home and in the local grocery shop and in the nearby drugstores The softcore pornography (or the kind of pornography that people refer to as softcore). '...) as I believe that I've already explained to you last night, the story goes in the early years of boys, we look around the back of the house and roads and the sideways of their communities, and frequently those who lived there would dispose of their garbage or whatever else they were doing to clean their home as well as, from time to time there would be pornographic magazines that were more of a hard kind of nature as opposed to, say, more graphic, let's be able to say,

7

more explicit type of material we'd find, say at your local store. It also contained items as Detective magazines." Similar to an account he shared to biographers who were not his, however at other times, he denies even having a fascination with detective books.

In the same way the man also spoke of his early moments as an Peeping Tom, and he believed himself as a social outcast. "I did not know the factors that made people tick. I was unsure of what makes people desire to become close friends. I wasn't aware of the factors that made people attractive. I wasn't aware of the factors that underlay interpersonal interaction." Unspoken is that staring at porn, or gazing through windows that are not fully covered does not mean that every teenager who is a predator. It's the same as experiencing social awkwardness does. There was clearly an additional sinister thought that was going on inside Bundy's head.

Bundy began to be involved in small criminal acts at an early age and was arrested several occasions However, despite the misdeeds, Bundy did not really make a splash in the positive or negative light in the school. Jim Adams, who attended his school alongside him, said, "I knew him because we had a number of friends who shared a common interest. One of them was Leonard Hoffman and, sometimes I'd go on rides with Leonard along with him Ted and Ted after school. They'd provide me with a ride back home, or they'd take me to eat some food or drink. This is what high schoolers tend to do. Leonard and I both were students in Latin class with each other, however he likely was a close friend to Ted. Ted was quite a person who was social during high school.

Someone who'd likely wear pants with a sweater, shirt and slacks and sometimes even wearing a tie. It seems like he was well-liked among the instructors because the class was well-organized as well as being well-liked by some of the most beautiful women. I recall that he had a female friend who took Latin class along with Leonard who was one of the most beautiful girls which was quite interesting to watch as they discussed his typical sort of girlfriend who and seemed attracted to...She was an incredibly beautiful brunette. It's hard to identify her now, however she was among the most gorgeous students in the class. I'm certain that she had a relationship with him for a short time. He seemed quiet, perhaps slightly reserved. do not know if he was shy. It seemed to me like he was comfortable, but perhaps it was a bit cautious. He was not as raucous than the majority of us."

Bundy as a senior in high school

Bundy completed his high school education in the year 1965. He attended the University of Puget Sound before moving for his first university, the University of Washington in 1966. He studied Chinese and was the typical student at college. Additionally, he was in a relationship with a girl identified only as Stephanie Brooks, but over time, he began to become less focused on his studies. After 1968, an event occurred that changed him. It appears that he started to believe the possibility that he was unnaturally born and the woman whom he believed to be his mother was actually his mother.

After the scandal, Bundy dropped out of school and started to shift around the city, from one job to another. In the meantime, he began to become more interested in politics, and was selected as a delegate for Washington to attend the 1968 Republican National Convention. In the end, the transformations Bundy went through became too to bear too much for Brooks and she split up with Bundy.

The tragedy was the last straw for Bundy after he quit Washington to explore in the United States, often visiting relatives and then confirm his doubts about his parents' lineage. In a strange manner, the revelation appeared to help reset his mind as he began an unplanned partnership and this time with a Utah divorcee who was named Elizabeth Kloepfer. After that, he re-entered University of Washington. University of Washington, where Kloepfer was employed as a secretary in 1970. He then changed his field of study to psychology.

He scored well and enjoyed the respect of the professors. He was also employed in his own Suicide Hotline in Seattle, with a former police officer whose name was Ann Rule, who would later publish what some consider as the most complete biographies about Ted Bundy.

In the wake of his graduation in 1972 of at the University of Washington, Bundy was a part of governor Daniel Evans' 1972 campaign to win reelection. The work he did with Governor Daniel Evans led to him being hired at the Washington State Republican Party as an assistant to the chairman and also he was accepted to law school at University of Puget Sound. University of Puget Sound.

Evans

Today, a successful young lawyer who seemed to be on the right path for an enviable job in politics, Bundy contacted

Brooks and began to date her. Both were discussing wedding, even though he was engaged with Kloepfer. At some point, he cut off contact with Kloepfer He explained the reason to later by saying "I just wanted to prove to myself that I could have married her."

In the next few months the student dropped out of law school, and started a new career as an infamous serial murderer.

Chapter 2: One of the Nation's Most Deadly and Notorious Serial Killers

"Extensive investigations were conducted and then the FBI swiftly began gathering information about Bundy's past criminal records and information about his identity. Then, FBI agents swore out an arrest warrant from the Federal government to stop unintentional escape to avoid being imprisoned and a cash reward of $100,000 was offered in exchange for the capture of Bundy. Bundy was not able to make it any further and was arrested at Aspen just a few days after. He stayed in Aspen and took advantage of another chance to escape during New year's Eve 1977, slipping through an open space within the ceiling of his cell, and getting out of the jailer's offices. The manhunt spread across the country and the FBI played an integral role. We constructed a number of posters for wanted and other identification materials processing latent fingerprints across the nation, and provided information via our Behavioral Analysis Unit as the days grew into weeks--re-joined Bundy to our Top Ten Desired Fugitives List on February 10th in 1978. Tragically, Bundy continued his murder rampage while in hiding. In the night on January 14th the 14th, he broke into the Florida State University sorority house and brutally killed two fellow students while leaving another suffering serious injuries. However, the net was shut. About the time of 1:30 a.m. on the 15th of February an Pensacola police officer spotted the stolen orange Volkswagen Beetle driving west on Cervantes Street and ordered the vehicle to stop. Bundy refused, but was arrested. Officers had no clue what was going on inside the vehicle however, Bundy was soon identified through the FBI's flyer identifying fugitive criminals. He returned to Colorado for trial on murder charges. Bundy was ultimately arrested and executed, however in the process of admitting over 2 dozen murders throughout the years. It is possible that there were some. Even to this day, Ted Bundy remains one of America's most dangerous and well-known serial murderers." The FBI Summary of the Bundy case

There is no way to know the first person who was Bundy's victim. Because of his reputation and confessions, he's suspect of several murders that he probably had nothing related to, like one which occurred in the year he was just fourteen years old. But, he was certainly harassing, raping, and killing women as early as 1974 after having researched and learned the strategies that he was aware of for acquittal of his crime. Kloepfer was later questioned by police and said that in the time period, "Ted went out a often in the evening. It was unclear exactly where he went. He also slept during the time. There were things I discovered, which I was unable to comprehend. An lug wrench that was placed halfway, underneath my car's seat. The man said it was to protect me. Plaster of Paris inside his bedroom. Crutches. The man had an Oriental knife inside a type of wooden case which was kept in the glove compartment in my vehicle. There were times when it was in the glove compartment. At times, it disappeared. The man had a meat cleaver. I watched him take it with him after he relocated to Utah. ... I questioned the man about [the plaster]

He told me that he had stolen it from the hospital supply store that he was employed at. He claimed he was unsure what the motive was. "Just to be silly about the matter,' he added. He claimed the crutches belonged to the landlord."

Actually, they are just some of the tools Bundy employed to kidnap and slaughter an innumerable number of teenage women. Some of his victims remain in the shadows even to this day. Karen Sparks was only 18 years old at the time Bundy entered her home and beat her on the face with a huge metallic object, then physically assaulted her using the same or identical object. As opposed to the other victims, she was able to survive even though she was barely able to survive and had severe brain injury.

Lynda Ann Healy who was the person who provided the daily ski forecast as well as an undergraduate in the University of Washington, was not the most fortunate. The same goes for Donna Manson, who became one of the youngest women to get noticed but just in a small manner. The 30th of March The Centralia Daily Chronicle featured a police note that stated, "Donna Gail Manson, an Olympia-based Student in The Evergreen State College, Olympia is missing since the 12th of March. The last time she was seen, she was wearing the red, orange and green striped shirt with green slacks, and a dark furry maxi-coat. Miss Manson stands five feet tall, weighs about 100 pounds, has long brown hair with blue eyes. Manson was featured this time on The Chronicle. This photo appears to be older. The Sheriff Don Redmond of Thurston County is requesting that all residents inform him of any suspicious activity. the office of Sheriff Don Redmond."

Before long, it became apparent that something odd was emerging within this region of Pacific Northwest. College students who were female, usually wearing dark, long hair with a middle split, started disappearing in a manner that was about one per month. On the 17th of April, Susan Elaine Rancourt went missing while Roberta Kathleen Parks disappeared on the 6th of May.

At this point, witnesses were coming to the scene with a variety of thoughts regarding what had happened however, a few testimony were particularly compelling. There was a rumor that two females recalled being approached by one man who seemed to be injured and asked them to assist to carry the book load to the car, which turned out to be the light-colored Volkswagen Beetle. Then, after Brenda Carol Ball disappeared, people came forward to say they saw her walk away along with a brunette-haired male with his arm tied in an strap. Then, a few days later Georgann Hawkins was also missing and left no trail of evidence to follow her. However, there several witnesses who claimed they saw an elderly man with crutches in her room in the evening. One of them also claimed that a man been spotted approaching her and asking for her help in carrying his briefcase, which was the exact kind of Volkswagen previously reported by witnesses.

The image shows Bundy's Volkswagen Beetle, which he employed to carry out a range of heinous acts, is displayed in the National Museum of Crime & Punishment

The most surprising aspect that can be seen in the past, particularly considering the modern day's 24/7 media cycle, is the fact it was not until the summer when newspapers started reporting there was something odd going on. In July 1st the Associated Press article noted, "Lynda Ann Healy disappeared without trace. The same is true for Donna Gail Manson, Susan Elaine Rancourt and Georgann Hawkins. Washington police officials, puzzled by the disappearances in the past six months of four college students from three universities who were missing, will be meeting tomorrow in Olympia to lay the foundation for a coordinated probe. The gathering, anticipated to bring together people from more than thirty law enforcement agencies across the state, is planned in conjunction with officials from Thurston County Sheriff's

Office which is responsible for the investigation in the case of Donna Gail Manson. ... Seattle homicide Lieutenant. Pat Murphy says he has no hint as to why the four disappeared. the missing four coeds. Additionally, there's no evidence of a crime committed in one of the cases Murphy says, even though each woman were deemed responsible for their actions and left behind a lot of belongings and clothing. "At this time, we can't find a suspect, even if there was one in hand,' Murphy said."

Then, the report continued to describe the events that took place to the ladies and the little details that the police could find. "Lynda Ann Healy who was 21 years old University of Washington senior, was last seen on the night of the 31st of January. 31 at the Seattle residence that she shared with four women. The bedroom in her basement room was

24

vacant the following day and there were bloody marks on her pillow. Donna Gail Manson, 19 is not ever seen since she bid goodbye to her three acquaintances and walked out of her dorm on the 12th of March. The student at Evergreen State College near Olympia had been heading for the jazz festival on campus. Susan Elaine Rancourt, 18 in Anchorage, Alaska, left the campus of Central Washington State College in Ellensburg at night on April 17, and was last reported to be walking towards her residence. Her clothing was still being washed in a dormitory washing machine and she was found missing on the following morning. Georgann Hawkins, 18, an University of Washington freshman, was last seen around 1 a.m. the 11th of June while walking through a dark alleyway towards her home at the Kappa Alpha Theta sorority house located in Seattle. Her disappearance was just 100 yards away from her location."

What did Bundy working at the time and, if not at the time of his shift? He worked for an agency called the Washington State Department of Emergency Services (DES) One of the agencies looking for women that he murdered previously. He also was dating Carol Ann Boone, who as Kloepfer was divorced.

Chapter 3: A Smooth Talking Man Named Ted

"One of the two missing women of Lake Sammamish State Park was last seen by a smooth talking' male known as Ted who was wearing an arm cast placed on his left arm. Police claim they were told by a person who was present. Mrs. Janice Ann Ott, 23. Issaquah she was last seen talking with the man in a tiny space on Sunday, at the huge picnic held by a beer. She left the picnic with the man after he agreed to build a sailboat for the car, according to police. The police have no leads to the disappearance of a second missing woman Denise Marie Naslund, 19. Seattle. Two women in Seattle did not meet, as police stated. ... King County Police stated that a female of 15 identified the man as smooth speaking. With a little British accent' and wearing an white T-shirt with White tennis shorts. Witnesses was able to hear the woman Mrs. Ott say, 'Well it's fine under one condition, to get me a ride aboard the sailing boat. The girl who disappeared put on her swimsuit and went away together with the man. Her bicycle went together with her. Her departure was around 12:30 p.m. The woman, named Miss Naslund was a part-time secretary was previously seen jogging towards the restroom. Police said that another person witnessed her exit the restroom as well as a third person reported seeing her walking to a different area in the park. The woman was in the restroom between 3:00 between 4 and 5:00 after 4. These women are among the six and seventh woman to vanish from the Northwest during the last few months. But, the police stated that there wasn't any connection between the disappearances the two women as well as five students missing from local schools and universities." The report is an Associated Press report, July 18 1975.

Bundy totally changed his strategy after the summer arrived, and kidnapped two women in the early hours on July 14, right on the beach area around Lake Sammamish State Park outside Seattle. The unfortunate two weren't the only ones who he attempted to contact. Five women later describe how they'd had been individually approached by Ted who addressed them individually and demanded for assistance in unloading the sailboat from his vehicle. Four, after hearing the police's warnings were hesitant to aid the man, another did agree, only to flee as she saw the sailboat was not aboard the car. However, Janice Anne Ott was not so savvy and went missing the same day as Denise Naslund.

Then, fear was beginning to take over all of the Pacific Northwest, as young women became concerned about becoming the next victim of a unknown killer. In a Sept. 6 Associated Press article, one campus security guard, Cheryl Martin, told the media, "Everyone's getting panicky now. Now we hear about girls who haven't contacted their boyfriends in the past week. Then we learn that it's easy like their phones are not working." In the same report, it was stated, "Coeds across the state fearful and police stalemated with a ghostly figure called 'Ted" in the disappearance of six college students. There are no bodies to be found. The police have not made any arrests. Police have looked over dozens suggestions and also delved into astrology and hypnosis as part of their search for concrete sources and potential suspects. However, if police were to meet 'Ted' on the next day and had no way to go further than simply inquire about the suspect. There's no evidence that links the cases apart from the fact the fact that all of them were beautiful, trustworthy and went missing in February, without leaving a trail. The parents who do contact us to report their daughters missing make calls much faster today,' explained Seattle Police Deb Margaret Oslin as they claim that their daughters have adopted a different way of telling people what they'll be doing. However, the teenage girls who went missing have also informed their friends of the plans they had."

Based on the information the police received from witnesses officers were able draw a picture of the suspect. this sketch appeared in every major newspaper within the region and was also frequently displayed on screens on television during news broadcasts. Kloepfer and Rule each contacted the police however their suggestions were not taken into consideration in many other suggestions that were received. The main issue that the police had to face was the fact that they did not have corpses to look at and in the end, they were not able to investigate the case as more than just suspicious disappearances. In all likelihood, the girls could have gone off with a bizarre polygamist they had been living happily in a different state. The people who thought there was a crime committed, they were not sure what kind of crime according to the report. to: "Thurston County Sheriff Don Redmond who is looking into missing Donna Manson from the Evergreen State College close to Olympia believes that the girls were sold into a slavery rings. A few other officers agree with his view but try to provide families with what is possible. ... The police are cautious when it comes to making connections between disappearances. However, Lieutenant. Richard Kraske of the King County homicide and robbery team believes that there is a possibility that the Ott and Naslund instances could be linked to the Rancourt incident. Two additional Ellensburg students, who are walking the exact same route that friends claim Susan Rancourt habitually traveled, have had encounters with young men with his arm in cast or sling, who demanded help in carrying his books into his Volkswagen. One of those encounters happened on 17 April, the day that Susan was missing. However, Kraske claims that the only factor that these cases do have in common is the fact that we don't have anyone. There may be a variety of individuals who are involved.'"

In the desperate attempt to find some information about what transpired Police even attempted ways of investigating that went out of their norms. According to the report, "Seattle police Capt Herb Swindler oversees investigations like the Healy and Hawkins probes. When he is involved in a case Swindler says, 'I'll accept anything that helps to solve the case.'" He's currently conducting research into psychics. Astrologers from two different astrologers told Swindler of a certain zodiac sign during disappearances. Swindler claims the pattern is comprised of every one of the Washington women, including an Oregon State coed, Roberta Kathleen Parks missing on in May 6 and Heidi Peterson,

4, missing in Seattle on Feb. 21. All of these disappeared while there was a moon that had remained in the fixed constellation in the zodiac. The other times, the signs was Pisces. Other times, the sign was split equally between Taurus or Scorpio. Swindler claims the pattern ended after there was no apparent disappearance on Aug. 4. Lt Kraske admits to being "sort kind of an agnostic moment' regarding the astrological and psychic patterns. However, he does state that one of the witnesses of The Lake Sammamish disappearances that included Naslund and Ott was subjected to two sessions of hypnosis and is in a state of confusion about additional information."

One of the items of evidence consistent with the police were looking at was Bundy's automobile that police had uncovered was the Volkswagen the newspaper called "an unique metallic hue that is a unique metallic shade of brown...King County detectives claim Volkswagen dealers have told them that this isn't the typical Volkswagen color, leaving the possibility of customized paint job. The VW distributor in British Columbia and Alberta says it hasn't been used in recent years neither. King County Detectives inspected the more than 400 VW registrations from different counties."

The piece concluded with a reference to the apparent heinous nature of the crime: "Dr. George MacDonald, clinical director of the sex offender section in Washington's Western State Hospital which houses about 150 people, told reporters that the staff has reviewed "Ted's" description and techniques against parolees as well as inmates. The check resulted in into no clues. King

County police say psychiatrists have put together a "character-profile that outlines what the character of "Ted" might look as. The police refuse to reveal the details, but claim they can use it to identify people who look like 'Ted' and don't behave like the profile suggests 'Ted is likely to. However, McDonald claims that the idea one can create a psychiatric report on someone who you've not had the pleasure of seeing is a myth. I've dealt with people who are deviant for 9 years, and I would not remove anyone from the basis of a report.'"

This was how the crimes, which led to interest beginning spreading beyond America's boundaries. The report concluded "Royal Canadian Mounted Police in nearby British Columbia say they have offered Washington police what aid they can--checking registrations on brown Volkswagen tips and forwarding bits of information."

The families of the victims continued endure with a ever-dwindling fire of optimism. Doctor. Donald Blackburn, Ott's father, said to reporters "I am hoping that nothing happens to our little girl. What do I hold on to? It seems that the idea that they are held in a place seems a bit improbable. It's not clear whether they're tied together however I think that it's feasible."

It was ironic that on the same day the article was released the two hunters located the remains from Naslund and Ott's remains. In September 11 the Associated Press story told readers, "Dental records have established that certain bones of a human discovered last week near Lake Sammamish State Park east of here, are remnants of two teenage females who vanished from the park around mid-July. Capt. J. N. Mackie confirmed yesterday that the remains were the remains from Denise Marie Naslund, 18 who was from Seattle and Janice Anne Ott, 23 from Issaquah. The two women disappeared on the 14th of July in Lake Sammamish State Park, 2 miles from the Issaquah location where the remains were found. Police believe the bones they found have been attributed to three people. University of Washington anthropology professor Dr. Daris Swindler said yesterday the additional four spinal bones as well one leg bone belonged to a third party. Mackie stated that neither the gender and age of the fourth person is known at this time. ... Police have said the identity of the remaining missing women is still a mystery. The authorities have said that Explorer Scouts will return on Tuesday to conduct a search in the area in which grouse hunters have discovered the bones on the previous day. "We have no way of knowing (how many remains are located at the site)." Mackie stated "That's why we're staying up there."

There were plenty of clues on the scene as well as the descriptions of the items found was horrifyingly horrific. "Some garments were discovered near the site where bones were found, however the police were unable to confirm the presence of weapons. The bones found to date were located in the air and the police believe that animals could be responsible for causing them to scatter. King Co. police Lt. Richard Kraske said there is a lot of coyotes living on the hills just outside Issaquah. Dr. Patrick Besant-Mathews is the King County medical examiner, stated yesterday that there was any evidence that a person intentionally cut the bones. In a situation such a case,' stated, 'you are thinking of animals first, and humans next.

If bones were cut completely through, it could suggest a person. The ends of a few of the long bones have been missing, and this is what an animal could be chewing. The police say that they do not know what caused the deaths of these women."

Other bones in the vicinity confirmed to be those of Hawkins. When there were dead body parts, the authorities knew without a doubt that they had the serial killer. But the thing they did not realize was that Bundy was already moving on to different hunting areas which was the

University of Utah, where the university had accepted him into the law school.

An image of the bedroom house in which Bundy was a resident of Utah

Chapter 4: The Circumstances Are Very Suspicious

"The two bodies of the deceased were discovered by a hunter on Saturday appeared to have been murdered, Clark County Sheriff Gene Cotton stated Monday. "We're still looking for an answer, but the facts appear to be very suspicious the Sheriff Gene Cotton stated. At this moment, believe that there was the possibility of homicide, said Cotton. Cotton added that he believes that the remains belonged to two women in their 20s and the bodies of their naked remains were within the woods for some time. But there is no indication that the remains were connected with the disappearances of a number of females in the college age group who were from Washington State this year. Cotton reported that about a dozen officers were continuing the hunt in the area to locate more bone fragments. Cotton reported that a hunter spotted an unidentified skull within the area on Saturday. Sheriff's office investigators later found two skulls, the lower jawbones as well as various bones. Sheriff's Sgt. Chuck Brink said long, fine hair that was dark and light brown was discovered in the vicinity. According to him, the hair as well as other features suggested that they were females and could be people aged between their late teens and the early 20s. The authorities believe that a vertebra discovered on the site could not be large enough to fit the skeletons that are partially reconstructed and could be an additional corpse. ... Clark County officials said that the hunt for other clues would be continued the next day. The bones found in the Issaquah as well as Yacolt cases were scattered while some appear to be chewed by animals. The King County police spokesman confirmed late on Sunday night that Lieutenant. Richard Kraske, who was in charge of the Naslund-Ott investigation, is in contact to Clark County Authorities. Sgt. Brink stated that he believes they were in the area around six months ago. Cotton stated that no clothes or personal belongings were discovered in the first search at this Clark County site." -- Associated Press article, October 1974.

In the beginning, Bundy was comfortable in his new environment and was seen with a variety of women. On the 2nd of October the 2nd, he abducted 16-year old Nancy Wilcox, whom he assaulted and strangled. The body of Nancy Wilcox was never discovered however, police were able to locate the body of 17-year old Melissa Smith, whom Bundy took just outside of Salt Lake City. In the night of

Halloween, he abducted 17-year old Laura Ann Aime, whose body was discovered in the morning of Thanksgiving Day, and on November 30, Salt Lake Tribune reported, "Lawmen from three Utah counties gathered on Friday in order to review information regarding the deaths of two 17-year-old teenagers, the disappearance an additional teen as well as the attempted kidnapping of two women over the past couple of days. Utah County Sheriff Mack Holley was in conversation with Capt. N. D. Hayward the chief of detectives at Salt Lake County Sheriff's Office; Midvalc Police Chief Louis S. Smith the dad of one of the murder girls, as well as Davis County Sheriff's deputies. Sheriff Holley stated that there are several leads being investigated and the relatives from Laura Ann Aime, whose body was discovered Wednesday morning in American Fork

Canyon, are seeking information on her activities. Her parents and grandparents, Mr. and Mrs. James J. Aime, Salem, told officers that they had last seen their daughter two weeks back. The doctor. Serge Moore, state medical examiner, stated that the girl was dead for about a week."

In the meantime there was a flurry of theories about the motives behind the murders and disappearances was being reported throughout the region and Hayward was determined to stop it. In the article "Capt. Hayward has sparked what he calls sick rumors' suggesting that the bodies of Laura Ann and Melissa Smith was discovered on October. 28 at Summit County, had been murdered. The victims were beaten severely or strangled, and then sexually assaulted however, they were not cut as he claimed. The search in search of Debra

Kent, 17 Bountiful and missing since November. 8. The law enforcement officials continued to interrogate the identity of a Murray girl as well as one Salt Lake County woman who claimed they were able to get away from the wrath of an abductor. There is evidence that suggests for the Smith and Aime murders were committed from the same group or the same parties, Sheriff Holley said. Capt. Hayward stated that officers are searching for a man who is six feet tall, who weighs 180 pounds with well-groomed dark hair, attractive and an expert dresser. Also, they are looking for a light-colored Volkswagen circa 1965 vintage that has rusty spots. Capt. Hayward stated that the horses and Jeeps will be searching all canyons of Salt Lake County Saturday to look for any missing girls turn up. He added that Davis County already has been conducted a thorough search. Sheriff Holley stated that no such search is scheduled to search for Utah County."

The most well-organized killers will commit a mistake. Bundy committed one on the night of November 8 in 1974, when he tried to abduct Carol DaRonch in Murray, Utah, who was able to escape and report the incident to the police. The newspaper reported the terrifying incident of Hayward's close call: "The DaRonch girl was freed after the person who kidnapped she veered off the roadway after placing a handcuff on one wrist. The other wrist cuff was 'loose. She managed to get out of the car, and sit in the middle of State Street near the mall under the light of an approaching vehicle, which was stopped by the police,' Hayward said. The abductor fled from there. The abductor drove an unmarked Volkswagen that had rust spots." Even though DaRonch was able to escape, Bundy was still so determined to get the freedom that he discovered in his crimes that he went to Debra Kent in the evening to murder Kent.

At this point, Bundy was a suspect of the crime, however those who saw Bundy in Lake Sammamish did not recognize the image of him the police had shown them. But, after Kloepfer called them back a second time, police took more notice of the details she shared. The most important information she could share information about the Bundy's activities and activities. She confessed "After I viewed the photos of 'Ted" in the newspaper back in July of 1974 I looked through the archives at the library to find the dates when the girls vanished as well as my calendar and cancelled check, but he was ... Well, there was no trace of him that time. ... A friendmentioned that the case cases in Utahare similar to those in the United States, and she told me that 'Ted' was living in Utah currently. Then I got in touch with my father and demanded that he connect with me from there. ... I'm still thinking about it and I'm praying that to find out. It's possible that I'm believing that one day you'll discover the truth. Ted and that it's somebody different ... however, in my heart, I'm not certain."

Kloepfer was also in contact with the police of Salt Lake City, becoming one of the very first to connect both different regions. In spite of her fears, Kloepfer still spent a time in the company of Bundy before returning to Seattle in the beginning of January.

After focusing his attention on teens, Bundy once again returned to killing women who were closer to his age the

12th of January, he abducted Caryn Campbell from Snowmass Village, Colorado. Just a few days after, United Press International reported, "A woman whose nude body was discovered in an abandoned snow bank on the side of the road was formally identified as the daughter of a Michigan resident, who disappeared just over one month ago during skiing with her husband. The deputy Ray Smith said the identification of Caryn Campbell was discovered through a post mortem conducted in Denver by using dental records. Investigators thought the victim was Miss Campbell since the body was discovered on Tuesday. There are suspects in the case that are being investigated,' Smith said. The cause of death is still unknown. of the death. Sheriff Carroll Whitmire was not available to comment at this time. The earring discovered near the body was initially recognized as belonging to Miss Campbell, but the investigators stated that a conclusive confirmation of the identity was not possible until a cross-check with Miss Campbell's dental records and mortuary records.

Whitmire stated that the body had been badly cut and was dragged by animal. The the wrist marks of the woman are still visible, and indicate she was bound to an automobile.

Sheriff said that the murder could be linked to a string of twelve other murders reported across the west United States. All of victims, including Miss Campbell, had shoulder length brown hair, parted down the middle with brown eyes.

Whitmire claimed that the body had not been found following Miss Campbell's disappearance in January. 12 at an Aspen skiing lodge, in which she was staying with her fiancé and doctor. Raymond Gradowski of Dearborn, Mich. The woman was last found when she left her doctor fiancee and other doctors at the entrance of the lodge in which they were staying in order to grab a newspaper from her second-floor bedroom."

Caryn Campbell

A photo of the hall in which Campbell was last seen.

On the 15th of March, Julie Cunningham disappeared, and just a few days later, Denise Oliverson joined the victims' list in April 6. Then Bundy's actions took on an additional sinister twist when he murdered 12-year old Lynette Culver, who was a victim of the murders in Pocatello, Idaho on May 6. Bundy killed Susan Curtis in late June Her body, as well as those of many of the others Utah victims, is not known till this day.

In the month of March, 1975, a small group of students on Taylor Mountain had come across an enormous collection of human remains, which later turned out to be belonging to the majority of the other Bundy victims.

In the meantime, Bundy was going about his usual business and was being with both Kloepfer and Boone, who both was still in contact with him, but also discussed a marriage with her, as well as Boone.

The couple was also seeing another woman whom he encountered during the law school. In the middle of summer of 1975, he was a member of The Church of Jesus Christ of Latter-day Saints and was baptized, although the church was not his primary focus. the church.

Chapter 5: Arrested Down There for a Traffic Violation

"He bought this book, the Joy of Sex book, at the time of his December 1973 birthday. He had read about a sexual encounter He was adamant about testing the method. It wasn't my cup of tea However, I still went with the guy.

There was a chapter in that book on bondage. He went straight into the drawer that I stored my nylons. He could tell what drawer it was. ... I'd never ever again do this.

The man didn't speak much about it, but he was very dissatisfied with me after I said, "No more.' ... At times, when I fell sleeping, I would awake and see him lying in bed. He was looking ... the body of my ... using an illuminated flashlight. ... When I mention cutting my hair], he becomes angry. He is a huge fan of the length of his hair.

One girl that I've ever seen-- and I'm sure of it-that he was with prior to me, has hair that is similar to my own. ... It's been a while since I've been able to catch him telling lies in numerous ways.

He claimed that the police had arrested him in connection with a traffic offense And I informed him that I could tell that was not an accurate account, as there'd be items found in the car which resembled tools used in burglaries.

The man said that they did not have any significance, and that it was a illegal search. ... I'm aware that he was the one who stole a TV in Seattle along with other things. Once, once, he said to me that if I told anyone else about the incident, the man would ... cut my neck."

The description of Kloepfer to police regarding her time in the company of Ted Bundy

"I have known people who ... radiate vulnerability. Their facial expressions say 'I am afraid of you'. These people invite abuse ... By expecting to be hurt, do they subtly encourage it?" The answer is yes. Ted Bundy in a 1977 note to Kloepfer

As Bundy was on the murder spree he was committing during his murder spree in Utah while police were in Washington continued to find a clue using a massive amount of data.

They decided that they needed to put all the data they could find into their massive payroll system and test whether the computer could detect any resemblances. The machine did, and Ted Bundy's alias showed in all the four lists produced. Ted Bundy was also listed in the top spot on the list of suspects but there was no tangible evidence that could justify his detention.

It was changed 1975 when a policeman stopped and pulled Bundy over in connection with a traffic violation, and then decided to investigate his vehicle.

He found an assortment of things the killer used to torture and kill the victims. Police took the case of Bundy and obtained an order for a search of his residence which led to the discovery of further evidence, but there was no enough evidence to warrant the suspect in custody.

However, the search wasn't thorough enough to find the pictures that he took and saved of his victims. These were found in the utility room. The police finally released Bundy however, they remained vigilant. They also questioned

Kloepfer who gave them details about some unusual objects she found within the house they discussed.

Ted Bundy's mugshot from 1975

The image below shows the things police found in Bundy's vehicle following his arrest in Utah

This was the moment when Bundy started to commit mistakes. After he had sold his vehicle to a local teen and the police took the vehicle and searched it carefully with hairs, which later were confirmed that they belonged to Caryn Campbell, Melissa Smith and Carol DaRonch.

Armed with this evidence they were able call him back and put his name in a list that included DaRonch, who identified the suspect as. The 3rd of October An Associated Press article reported, "A

University of Utah law student was arrested on Thursday for an aggravated kidnapping as well as attempted criminal killing in connection with an incident that occurred on Nov.

8 of a 17 year old girl claiming that a person posing as a police officer kidnapped the girl at Fashion Place Mall in Murray. ... The suspect named in the complaint of two pages as the suspect was Theodore Robert Bundy, 28 .... He was taken into custody on Thursday night following questioning the suspect by Salt Lake County Sheriff's Capt. N. D. Hayward as well as other law enforcement officers. ... Murray Police Sgt. Paul Forbes, who signed the complaint, alleged that the said Theodore Bundy...did deliberately or in a shrewd manner, using the use of force, threats or deceit to detain or detain Carol DaRonch contrary to her own will

in order: (a) To facilitate the commission or attempted the commission of a crime, which includes the crime of homicide, or an aggravated assault and (b) to cause injuries to or intimidate Carol DaRonch.

The second count claims that the accused '...attempted to purposely or recklessly result in her death even though the defendant was in the perpetrator of or attempted to carry out the aggravated crime of kidnapping or kidnapping.

The complaint further says that the defendant "has been recognized by Carol DaRonch as the one who took her with deceit or force at in the Fashion Place Mall at 6100 S. Slate in Murray and pointed a firearm towards her, and said he was planning to blow up her head.'"

In the year 2000, according to the report, Bundy was "a second-year law student

[and] a part time custodian at the university." The article also stated "In Oiympia, Wash. An aide Lieutenant. Governor. Daniel J. Evans confirmed the report that Bundy was an 'assistant to the campaign' of Governor John McKinley." Republican chief executive, but wasn't a salaried employee of governor.

Washington University daily newspaper personnel confirmed that Bundy graduated from the school in 1972, earning an undergraduate degree in psychology.

According to the Associated Press reported from Seattle Thursday night Bundy was the assistant director of the Seattle Crime Prevention Commission in 1973.

In that year, he was the subject of publicity after it was reported that he caught a purse-snatcher. AP added that Bundy was previously an assistant for The Washington State Republican Central Committee."

In the wake of the arrest of Bundy, his parents offered him a bail of $15,000 He was subsequently housed in the home of Kloepfer until the time of his trial.

In November, the investigators who were in charge of the murders that took place in Washington, Utah and Colorado were reunited and decided that Bundy could be the person they had all been looking for however, they required more proof before they could accuse him.

After he had waived his rights to be tried by a jury, Bundy was convicted on March 1st, 1976 of charges relating to DaRonch and sentenced to 15 years of the Utah State Prison. Bundy attempted to flee at the end of October, but he was arrested.

Meanwhile, Colorado finally felt it was able to prove him with murder in the case of Caryn Campbell. He was put in the state in the beginning of January.

But he was determined not to have the chance to appear in court. rather, he put his energy into preparing his escape at the time he had the chance to escape, he did so.

In June 1977 The Associated Press reported, "Accused murderer Theodore Bundy escaped from custody this morning by leaping from the second floor window of the Pitkin County Courthouse during a break in the pretrial hearing. ...[Hewas able to escape in the course of a hearing regarding the motion filed by him in order to abjure the death penalty in case the jury finds him guilty.

The defense attorneys who assisted Bundy have concluded their argument in court, when District Court Judge George Lohr declared a recess prior to hearing the defense's response. The sheriff's office claimed that Bundy was seen jumping from the window during recess, and ran through the courthouse towards the Roaring Fork River."

A photo of the courthouse, from which Bundy was able to escape by jumping from the second story window first from left

The residents of Aspen eagerly waited throughout the next week, worried that a psychotic murderer was in the area however, Bundy didn't make it to the scene before being nabbed after six days. As the Associated Press reported, "Bundy 30, who was arrested early on Monday morning by sheriff's deputies. They took down a stolen 1966 Cadillac in the town of Aspen. The deputies said that the driver collapsed and sped off the road while their vehicles of patrol drove by. Bundy felt extremely tired and could not think any more according to the sheriff's department claimed, and complained that he had only gotten 10 hours of rest since his escape. He was allowed to lie down the afternoon of Monday in a cell located in the basement of the courthouse.

Following a questioning of Bundy the sheriff's department claimed that he had spent at least 10 miles from Aspen after his escape on Tuesday. ... The sheriff's sergeant Don Davis, said Bundy was asked about the reason he fled and he replied, 'I did not wish to return to prison.

It was simply too gorgeous out there.' Davis said Bundy was also able to tell him that he'd sought out an opportunity to flee. He did it through a second-floor windows in the back of the courtroom after being it was left open during a break in the pretrial hearing.

"I think Ted got a bit of satisfaction because he was able to get to the extent he could in the end,' explained Davis. Bundy was walking with a limp when he was before the court on Monday.

The sheriff's department announced that the doctor will examine a knee that he was injured during his leap to escape."

The report later detailed the escape route of Bundy in the manner the police had asked him to explain it.

officers "Bundy left east of the courthouse following his escape. He ascent Aspen Mountain before dropping into Castle Creek, about 10 miles to the south from Aspen, Davis said. After that, he spent a few days in a deserted cabin Davis claimed, before he complained of being alerted to the presence of the sound of a helicopter searching. Bundy said he'd obtained the .22 Caliber rifle from the cabin, the department of sheriff stated, however he claimed to have put it away in the forest after he became exhausted of taking it with him. The suspect was not in armed custody when he was arrested arrest, and did not resist an official from the department of sheriff stated. District Attorney Frank Tucker said Bundy would be accused of felony escape, second-degree burglary and misdemeanor stealage for the rifle he allegedly took, as well as felony theft for using the vehicle which he was driving on the day he was arrested."

The image used to illustrate an FBI's Ten Most Wanted Fugitives

Chapter 6: Kimberly Diane Leach

"On the 9th of February in 1978 Kimberly Diane Leach, age 12, was taken into the Lake City Junior High School which was located at Duval Street (U. S. Highway 900, Lake City, Columbia County, Florida by her mother, Freda Leach, at around 8:15 a.m. It was a cold and wet morning. Following a group of schoolmates The Leach girl was off to her class in the homeroom about 8:15 a.m. The homeroom class was within the Central Building. Her teacher for homeroom was John Lawrence Bishop. Within fifteen minutes of attending school, the bell rang to signal the beginning of class of the day, which in the case of Leach's daughter included Physical Education. Due to the weather conditions pupils gathered in the auditorium to enjoy movies, rather to playing outside. In order for Leach to get the Leach girl to travel to her classroom at home located in the Central Building to the auditorium the school had to let her out of at the back of the school building, then go out, wander around mobile buildings and then through the basketball courts which is approximately 247 feet to get into the auditorium. When she left from the classroom and returned to the classroom, Ms. Bishop noticed that she was unable to retrieve her purse. He sent her classmate, Tandy Bonner, to the auditorium, to transport Leach back in her homeroom to get her purse. Leach was able to, indeed go out of the auditorium at the consent of her teacher in Physical Education Mrs. Juanita Caldwell, returned to Mr. Bishop's classroom, and stole her purse. After she left her class to go back to the auditorium, she was between 9:20 a.m. until 9:25 a.m." - - A court filing pertaining to the appeal filed by Bundy in his conviction of the Kimberly Leach murder

After his return to the custody of his family members, people close to Bundy suggested Bundy to stay in custody and stand trial even though he had planned to be the sole attorney for himself, which is which is a well-liked but usually unwise option for defendants in criminal cases. There is a good chance that Bundy could have escaped during the trial, but Bundy was determined to get out yet again, and he began to work on his plan of escape that he put into action at night on December 30th in 1977. The next day it was reported that the Associated Press relayed the story about Bundy's escape from the Garfield County Jail: "Theodore Bundy...escaped Saturday from the Garfield County Jail by crawling through the cell's roof. .... The Undersheriff

Robert A. Hart said Bundy was in his cell just after noon on Saturday. Bundy has been last observed inside his cell around seven p.m. the previous Friday. Hart stated that Bundy was believed to have walked through the hole through the wall where a light fixture been, and then entered the prisoner's residence, and went out of the building. Police immediately began a investigation. ... The officials reported that Bundy was set for transfer into Colorado Springs, where his trial was moved due to an alteration of the location. Bundy is set to appear for trial on the month of Jan. 9. Hart told the court that Bundy...left blankets unrolled inside his bed so that it appeared like he's in bed."

The thing that the media didn't mention was that, when Bundy left in the morning, he had $500 worth of cash, which was given to Bundy by Boone. The press also did not reveal that he'd been absent for over 17 hours, before the prison authorities discovered his location and at this point, he'd robbed an automobile and, when it had broken down, he made his way via hitchhiking, bus and a bus to Denver which is where he caught the plane that took him that took him to Chicago.

Bundy didn't stay in Chicago for long, but instead he made his route to Florida and soon began to return to his former habits. In January of 1978 it was reported that the United Press International reported with shock, "Two Florida State University students were strangled to death in their dormitories while three students were brutally beaten, but then rescued on Sunday morning by a club-wielding killer, who entered through an open door. One of the girls was assaulted. One of them was hospitalized in critical condition. Police Chief Ken Katsaris said the assailant who he described as 'depraved appeared to be an unknown to girls who were within Chi Omega. Chi Omega sorority house. The incident put students on the campus in a state of fear. Police placed a 24-hour security guard at Chi Omega's Chi Omega residence and stepped the security of the entire campus which is located about a dozen blocks away from downtown Tallahassee as well as the capitol of the state. One of the survivors in the house of sorority said her assailant was an ungainly white man who was in his early twenties. The deceased girls, having their own space at the top of Chi Omega, were identified as Chi Omega house, were identified as Lisa Levy, 20 of St. Petersburg, a student in the fashion industry as well as Margaret Bowman,

21, from St. Petersburg, a senior majoring in art history."

What was made clear in the report was the fact that Bundy was involved in things that were completely different from before he attacked girls inside the building, and then abandoning their bodies.

And then there was the question of the three survivors. The writer explained that "Injured during the incident were two roommates in the sorority Karen Chandler of Tallahassee, who is a senior economics major as well as Kathy Kleiner, 21, from Miami Both are listed as being as in good health in Tallahassee Memorial Hospital. Cheryl Ann Thomas. 22, from Richmond, Va., A sophomore majoring in dance was unconscious when she was assaulted within a duplex just six blocks away from the house of sorority.

The victim was in critical situation. "We've got an absolute nut in this area,' claimed Jim Sewell, deputy security officer of the police on campus. The students were evicted from Chi Omega's Chi Omega home following the murders and stayed with their friends who live in the town. The victims passed away from strangulation however Katharsis claims that the assaults were so severe that they could have resulted in death. There is no evidence of conflict and the victims were assaulted unconscious and then were strangled. A few, possibly more, was raped, said the source. It was a terrifying scenario."he told reporters. I don't believe they realized what happened to them.'"

The police later discovered that Chi Omega attacks were Chi Omega attacks took place in a short period of time, and they were extremely brutal. Bundy continued to get more out of control and was becoming reckless. Police were also able to find evidence that was physical inside Thomas the bed, which could be linked to Bundy.

Two of Bundy's victims who were his last.

For humanity's sake, Bundy's murder spree was close to a conclusion. On February 8, 1978 he drove off to Lake City, Florida, in which he abducted and murdered 12 year old Kimberly Leach from her school. The next day the car was stolen and drove westward into the Florida Panhandle. However, after having been on the road for three days was arrested by an Pensacola Police officer. In the Associated Press story published on 17 February "The strange incident started Wednesday at around 1:30 a.m. at which point Pensacola police officer David Lee stopped a man who was driving a VW bus that was discovered as stolen in Tallahassee in the previous month. The driver attempted to escape out of the vehicle following an intense chase, and Lee shot two times before the suspect was taken into custody. The city's jail prisoner identified himself in the form of Kenneth Raymond Misner, 29 from Tallahassee. He was carrying Misner's identity papers as well as a handful of counterfeit credit cards the police claimed. The real Kenneth Misner, a former FSU track player, quickly was identified in Tallahassee which is where he's studying at a graduate level. The detectives noticed a hint the evening of Thursday, that their suspect was Bundy according to the detective Norman Chapman. After two hours, FBI agents arrived with wanted posters, fingerprints and wanted signs."

Bundy was arrested after being detained in Florida in 1978.

When Bundy is in jail, scores of police officers as well as individuals were scouring the Florida forest for Kimberly Leach. Then, on April 7 the body was discovered. According to court papers, "On February 11, 1978, a photograph taken of Kimberly Diane Leach, her details, as well as the circumstances surrounding her disappearance surfaced in news outlets of the state and local including television and press. In the next few months, an investigation of the size and scope that was unheard of in the books of Florida the past was undertaken to find the missing woman. The task force, which was around 100 members at any time was en massed, and nearly every square inch in Columbia County, and surrounding counties was uncovered by the group. The hunt was conducted by a high-ranking group of police officers. They were assisted by the Assistant State Attorney George Robert Dekle, of the Third Judicial Circuit State Attorney's Office. The 7th of April, 1978, when a members of the search team went through a wooded area in close proximity to Suwannee River Suwannee River in Suwannee County, Florida, one of the participants of the search team, Florida Highway Patrol Trooper Kenneth W. Robinson stumbled on a tin hog barn. When he sat down, he scanned into the shed, he noticed the an unidentified human body as well as a heap of clothing. Trooper Robinson called all the members of the search team. The search area was then cordoned off in anticipation of the arrival from the State Medical Examiner and Anthropologist and The Florida Department of Law Enforcement Crime Lab Team and personnel from the State Attorney's Office, and the investigators who are in charge of Kimberly Diane Leach's disappearance. Kimberly Diane Leach."

Chapter 7: Evidence of Guilt

"The significance of the probative effect of flight evidence in the form of circumstantial evidence to prove guilt was analyzed in the Fifth Circuit Court of Appeals according to the level of trust with which four possible inferences are taken: (1) from the defendant's conduct leading to the flight; (2) from flight into guilt consciousness; (3) from consciousness of guilt, to a sense of guilt regarding the crime being committed; as well (4) from a sense of guilt regarding the offense charged to the an actual conviction for the offense charged. ... There are none of the flaws that would render the evidence used in this case unadmissible. The time that Bundy was captured in Pensacola following his escape from the policeman who had arrested his escape, it took place six days since the Leach girl disappeared. Her disappearance was the subject of much media attention and that it's reasonable to suggest the assumption that Bundy ran away from the police because he was aware of guilt of the Leach incident. It was also only two days after the Leach murder that Bundy ran away from officer Dawes when Dawes discovered the license plate that was on the floorboard of the vehicle Bundy was believed to be using. It's reasonable to think for a jury to infer the circumstantial evidence as an evidence of guilt. We conclude both of the incidents are admissible as pertinent evidence that a jury might utilize as evidence circumstantial to prove guilt." In this excerpt, we discuss the ruling of a judge on an appeal by Bundy.

A photo of Bundy walking out of the Miami courtroom

Bundy was accused of the murder of Kimberly Leach, but he didn't go to trial at the time. In June 1979, instead Bundy was taken to Miami to face trial over those who died during Chi Omega. Chi Omega case. The shift in the location was prompted because of the acclaim generated by this case. As the trial started He insisted once more that he represented himself. However, he was in a bid to avoid the spotlight of over 200 journalists who were sent around the globe to write about the trial.

One of the first American trials to be shown on TV, Bundy preened and strutted before jurors, mostly disregarding the counsel of his counsel appointed by the court and committing a total blunder of any defense that was available. Bundy even resisted the plea bargain which would have handed him 75 years in prison instead of an electric chair. It was simply too difficult for him to admit that he was guilty of anything.

Odontologist Richard Souviron who was a witness to an odontological bite mark that was discovered on Levy

Bundy on trial in 1979

The prosecution was able to present a convincing case, although many think that it was more likely that Bundy did not let his lawyers manage the matter, he may be exonerated. There were two Chi Omega sisters, Connie Hastings and Nita Neary, both admitted to being near his home in the evening. In addition is the bite marks on the left buttock of Levy was shown to match the teeth of Bundy.

In spite of the evidence he was presented with during his closing arguments, Bundy told the jury, "I'm not asking for mercy because I think it ridiculous to seek mercy on something that I didn't commit. This is the opening line of my argument. This is an initial round, two rounds, the beginning of a lengthy battle and I'm not giving up at all. It's my belief that if I'd capable of presenting the evidence that supports my innocence -- which actually, in my opinion, has created reasonable doubtand had an effective representation, I'm sure that I'd be exonerated, and, should I be granted an appeal, is likely to be found not guilty. It was difficult to go through the trial due to various reasons. The main reason why the trial wasn't simple in the beginning of the case was due to the public presentation of the evidence regarding what transpired within Chi Omega House. The Chi Omega House, the photographs, the blood and the blood-stained sheets. Also, to realize that the state wanted to track me down to be accountable wasn't easy. This was no easy to overlook the parents of these girls. They are not my friends. But I'm not sure that it's a sin for me God knows what, to claim that I am in their shoes, as best I can. It's the first time this kind of thing has occurred to anyone near to me. However, I'm informing the court, and the people who are who are close to the victims in this instance: I'm certainly not accountable for the crimes committed at Chi Omega House or Dunwoody Street. Chi Omega House or Dunwoody Street. The court will also hear that I'm unable to believe the verdict since, even though the jury was a part of the verdict that these violations were committed, it was a mistake in determining who was responsible for these crimes. In the end, I'm not able to accept the sentence, even if it will be handed down and I am aware of that the legal way in which the judge will decide to impose itas it's not a punishment I personally received. It's a sentence imposed by another person who isn't in this courtroom this moment. Therefore, I'll be savagely punished by and suffer the consequences due to that crime ... however, I'm not sharing the blame or guilt. ... and now it's on the justice system. It's not my fault. This court looks like an aquatic hydra in the present. The court is being asked to show none mercy, just as the madman in Chi Omega House. Chi Omega House dispensed no mercy. You're asked to think about this matter as a human and judge. You're also asked to give the wisdom of gods. This is like a fantastical Greek tragic play. It was probably created at some point and be among those old Greek plays which depicts the man's three faces."

Despite all the efforts of Bundy received a summary conviction on the 24th of July 1979, and sentenced to the death penalty. One of the more famous sentences in American legal history the judge Edward Cowart said, "It is ordered that you are executed with a current of electric which will traverses your body until dead. Be careful you young man. I advise you sincere. Be careful of your health. It's tragic for this jury to see an utter waste of human life I've seen in this chamber. You're a bright young man. You'd be a great lawyer. I'd wanted to see you do your work before meBut you chose a different direction, dear your partner. Be careful of your health. There is nothing I dislike toward you. I would like you to understand that."

Bundy's post-Chi Omega conviction photo.

After six months of the Chi Omega conviction, Bundy was taken to Orlando to be tried for Leach's murder. The way he behaved during the trial was much more volatile as compared to his Chi Omega proceedings. As per the Associated Press story in February 1980, "Bundy called his fiancee, Carole Boone, as his sole and first witness. He began with a request to describe to the jury what kind of relationship that we've enjoyed. She. Boone, A twice-married mother of a boy who was 15 years old told the court that they had met when they worked for a state government agency located in Washington state back in 1974. It grew into a more serious romantic type of relationship and she explained. "Sometimes, I'd like to get married, but only if it goes well. He's a kind, warm compassionate man who is a good friend,' Mrs. Boone told the jury. I would like to see you return with a life sentence rather than death. In an examination re-direct by Ms. Boone that Bundy declared they were legally married. "I'd like to state this in a very precise manner that I am married,' he added with a solemn tone. "Will you be my bride?' 'Yes marry you,' Ms. Boone said. "I do now hereby wed you and I do hereby marry you,' Bundy said. "Thank you. In a tearful closing argument before jurors, Bundy stated to the jury that the couple was married. Boone married because 'it was the sole chance to sit in the same room with the words that were able to be exchanged. The woman. Boone applied for a marriage license on Tuesday last week to get married Bundy and it's not permitted in prison policies to allow people who are in prison to marry. Jopling and defense attorneys put away any inquiries about whether or not the Bundy declaration in a legal court was the wedding."

In the end, the union was legally valid according to Florida laws because their marriage declarations were made before the judge. Within a couple of hours, Bundy was convicted of murdering Leach and was sentenced to his third execution.

A mugshot of Bundy following his conviction for the murder of Leach.

Bundy was within his Florida jail system for the next nine years after his conviction. In that time, he was surrounded by friends with regular visits by Boone and with whom it is possible that he secretly had an infant. Also, he spent a good portion of his time talking to biographers and enjoyed the attention of others as he shared with the story of his personal account. He often talked about his joy when he held onto items which he stole from people around him, telling a reporter, "The big payoff for me was in the possession of whatever it was that I stole. This wasn't about the crime that was the main thing. At times, I'd have the desire to be drunk to get relaxed enough to carry out the task in a proper manner. Other than that it was really fun to have an item on my desk or in my home which I'd wanted but went out to get." He claimed that the attacks he made at his victims elicited the same intense feeling of being in being in possession.

If he wasn't being interviewing, Bundy spent his time looking for a way to escape. A failed escape attempt was stopped by guards in July 1984, when they were able to see that he cut one of the bars inside the window of his cell. Bundy gave his tips to police officers who were looking into other murders suspected to be serial and the infamous Green River Killer, of who Bundy warned, "This guy is responsible for another twenty-three deaths, at the very least." He also said that there's a sense of possessiveness that is evident in this. This is a method of explaining it in fairly simple terms: a possession that allows the dead to be just as valuable as a living victim in certain aspects. It's the physically possessed and owned or taking or taking it's just one aspect of the disorder. The feeling of power and ownership is one of the primary reasons for me to believe that in some situations, though not always--is the reason I suspect that he is at least in a sense planning to return on the scene in order to observe his victim or even engage with the body in any manner."

The date of his initial execution was nearing, the one in connection with Chi Omega murders, Chi Omega murders Bundy started to admit to not solved murders. He also admitted particulars of the actions he committed to bodies following the bodies had been dead. The execution was delayed on appeal and a variety of others until finally, Florida Governor Bob Martinez approved a death sentence. The execution date was on January 24, 1989, for his murder. Kimberly Leach.

As death is now imminent, Bundy was able to meet with police officials and admitted to killings he'd committed within Washington state and in the zone. Bundy also admitted to numerous murders that he had committed, some of the women's names that they may not have heard of. The truth soon came out that he kept the details hidden hoping that it could earn him a second stay in order to reveal more. It didn't work so Governor Martinez insists, "We are not going to allow the system to be manipulated. The fact that he is negotiating to save his life with the dead bodies of the victims is a sham."

In the night prior to his death, Bundy pulled off one famous act of sheer ego through arranging an interview with the renowned Christian psychology expert Doctor. James Dobson. People around the world listened with horror at the recorded interview, where Bundy claimed that his actions were due to having been exposed to pornography at an early age. Bundy acknowledged, "I don't want to end up dying. I'm not going on to fool you. We won't be fooling you. I'm sure that I'm worthy of the harshest punishment that society has...I believe that society should be shielded from me and other people as me...well that's a good thing. People will be able to condemn the behavior of the Ted Bundy when they pass magazines that are full of exactly the kind of stuff that cause young children into the future to become"Ted Bundys."

The news conference resulted in Dobson international attention, and also sparked denigration, with many believing that Bundy is once again manipulating the system to obtain the results he desired. Responding to critique, Dobson asserted, "I didn't oppose the execution. I believe he was deserving of it. I have never told Ted that he didn't have the right to die. I believe I was quite honest with him on this. If there was a circumstance in which an individual should receive the highest penalty I'm sure he got it. .....I'm not a defender to Ted Bundy."

It turned out that the meeting with Dobson was his final chance for promotion himself. That day, at 7:16 a.m. in the morning of the 24th January in 1989, Bundy passed away in an electric chair in the Florida State Prison located in Raiford, Florida. Eleanor Rose, the mother of the victim Denise Naslund, may have put it in words people's emotions most effectively when she stated, "For everything he did to the girls-the bludgeoning, the strangulation, humiliating their bodies, torturing them - I feel that the electric chair is too good for him."

A photo of Bundy one day before his execution

Ted Bundy was dead, however the long shadow it cast was far from disappearing, as was pointed out by Belva Kent, who was the mother of the victim Debra Kent "He ruined our lives and he's still part of your life, unfortunately." Even when the consequences of the crimes committed by Ted Bundy remain in the news to this day, experts and people continue to discuss what drove him to commit the crimes he did. In a debate about the exact quantity of victims Bundy killed, the Reverend Fred Lawrence, who gave Bundy the last rites of his execution, declared, "I don't think even he knew ... how many he killed, or why he killed them. That was my impression, my strong impression." Detective Robert Keppel, who meticulously examined the list of victims along with Bundy himself, said, "A long-term serial killer erects powerful barriers to his guilt, walls of denial that can sometimes never be breached." Ted's mother was also trying to confront the crimes her son was responsible for during an interview before the executionthat "If he killed all those lovely young women-we have several beautiful daughters of our own, we know how we would feel and its a terrible thing. And he wasn't raised that way! He was raised in a good, loving, caring family. Dang it! We still love and care for him, but we want to know: what caused this?"

At the end of the day, detective Keppel was the one who spent a lot of time with Bundy could have stated Bundy the best way in a single assertion: "He's definitely a premier serial murderer. It's likely that he's the perfect model. There aren't any other model similar to him. Fortunately."

Chapter 8: The Drifter

When Ted Bundy entered adolescence he started to experience some amazing growth spurts, both academically and physically. He would often be ahead of his class and around one head higher than the rest of his classmates. He was awarded A's and even B's. He convinced his mother that he was a special child possibly her only child with the potential to be capable of rising above the petty, working class roots. He pinned her dreams of getting a college degree--one that she never could get for herself, upon Ted's shoulder.

Her constant presence was a supporter for Ted to continue his studies after he graduated of Woodrow Wilson High School, it was evident that it been rewarded when he got confirmation that he was granted a scholarship to the world-class University of Puget Sound in

Tacoma, Washington. Following his high school graduation, Ted began working work as a summer employee in the city, and appeared to be waiting to see the potential that was waiting for his in Puget Sound.

However, this stunning painting of Ted Bundy's perfect time off prior to beginning his university years is shattered by the suspicion. Even even though Ted wasn't charged in any of his crimes, at the time he began his final year at high school he was suspect in several burglaries. At the time he finished his school year of 1965, Ted was the most likely suspect for a variety of crimes. While he wasn't legally accused, his name was private in the files of juvenile courts, possibly as a hint of what was to follow.

However, the opportunities were not pursued in any way, and he ended up being allowed to go to the world-class University of Puget Sound that autumn, just as he had scheduled. In Puget Sound Bundy continued to excel academically, but soon he started to experience a feeling of a crippling lack of confidence within his group, and not but he felt that his social skills were somewhat sluggish when compared with other students, but he felt physically "outclassed" by his associates who came from wealthy family backgrounds whereas Bundy came from moderate, working class backgrounds.

Thinking he'd never ever be able to integrate into the higher crust of society in Puget sound, Bundy used his good marks he earned as a way for transferring to the University of Washington where he decided to pursue a degree in Chinese. Ted was a bit of a nerd and had an interest in the Chinese language and thought that China as a rapidly growing global power was an important place to get familiar with. While in The University of Washington Ted initially was in a dorm named "McMahon Hall."

The dormitory was where Ted met his first love of his life; A woman just a couple of years older than him and whose name was Stephanie Brooks. Although Ted was enthralled by Stephanie, he was at the beginning extremely intimidated by her. He was feeling overwhelmed and totally unprepared when it came to her attractiveness and taste for males. It was apparent that she appeared to naturally tend to attract top performers students and high-class men, much to the delight of Ted Bundy seemed to leave the man "outclassed" once again.

It was as if the unhappy and depressed Ted Bundy was relegated to observe his lover from the distance. Then he came to the breakthrough. He was able to see that there was a common interest that they shared -- he realized that both of them loved skiing. The topic of skiing was that Ted came up with a method to talk and also to worm his way into Stephanie's world. To Ted's delight, she seemed to be much more than willing. In the end, she gave him a ride into the popular Ski Resorts which dotted the Seattle area.

The two soon bonded in the years following they quickly became friends, and Stephanie was soon to become Ted Bundy's first love. After turning 20 Ted was caught trapped in the all-consuming, emotional turmoil of first love. bring. After that, even from the dark confines in his prison cell being on Death Row, he would remember that time of shining sunshine that he had experienced as the best time of his life. Stephanie had been as a guide as his love and he was awestruck by her, soaking up the joy which she shared with him.

Another person with a history that was wealthy and high-class, and for Ted the thought was that maybe she was the person who could finally lift him out of the pit of being mediocre. He imagined the best of her and wanted to grasp her and hold to the hope of happiness which he believed she could give him. However, it was kind of clinginess which would ultimately cause her to leave. Ted Bundy was a young Ted Bundy seemed to have an emotional gap which he would like Stephanie to help fill. However, the need was greater than Stephanie could ever do to his needs.

As well as his low levels of happiness, Ted Bundy was also financially strapped during this time as well and was forced to take on at a variety of low-paying jobs in order to afford his lodging and meals in the University of Washington. That meant he did not have a lot of money to go out with Stephanie which meant that he was forced to limit the time to picnics, walks in the parks, perhaps a film. At the start, Stephanie did not seem to be averse her gentle manner. It was a sharp contrast to his more violent behavior, as well as the devoted attention that he lavished on his daughter.

As Stephanie approached graduation, and Bundy appeared to be stuck in the 2nd stage, never quite making his way through life She became more doubtful of any possible future in their friendship. After her graduation, in 1968, she was determined to inform Ted the same thing. In addition, she was hoping that their constantly changing situations would assist her in ending the affair. Following graduation, she had plans returning to her hometown of California for a job.

The girl figured out that because Ted was in the midst of a sophomore slog in his studies, this could be the anchor she required to keep from catching him. It seemed to her that the inevitable limitations of distance and time could do all the heavy lifting for her. However, when Ted stunned her at the final minute with an award to take classes in Mandarin (Chinese) within the highly regarded California Ivy League school of Stanford to study for the duration of season, Stephanie's dreams to construct a wall for distance were shattered. The dorm room of Stanford Bundy was practically down the road from the place where Stephanie was staying within San Francisco.

Even when the couple renewed their love during the summer, Stephanie finally did manage to end their relationship in the end when she learned that Ted's course in Mandarin was finished and he had to go back to Seattle's University of Washington in Seattle. Ted Bundy was absolutely heartbroken. While in the grips of depression and anxiety the man was struggling to focus on his studies and his academic performance began to decline. In despair of being unable to anymore function, he dropped out completely from school. Ted quit Washington state Washington completely and headed east to spend most of 1968 and the majority of 1969 at the home of his family members in Pennsylvania.

There, Bundy set out to discover his ancestors and verify the things he'd long believed to be true. In his belief that his lack of self-worth stemmed from the fact that he was not a legitimate person He sought out the reasons for the birth of his son. The result was that he could finally discover the birth certificate. On this official certificate which he was able to hold in his palm, was the name of a woman that he'd long dreamed to be the "sister" listed to be his mother. The thing he'd always suspected could be true.

The father, on his part, turned out to be a largely unknown person, identified as a man whose name was Lloyd Marshall. All he could get from the man was that he had been the son of a Penn State grad, an Air Force vet and a faint remark that his father later was a salesperson. Did he know who the father of his was? An entrepreneur who went door to door selling his products? Did his mother know how she was introduced to the person? Could he be the result of any completely random trip of an artisan with two bits?

The thoughts were to keep haunting Ted Bundy for the rest of his existence, and Ted Bundy never was able to overcome the bitter feeling of loss that he felt over the fact that he didn't know his father. The feeling of betrayal towards his father was only amplified by the constant feeling of guilt he had towards his former girlfriend Stephanie Brooks. At this point when he wrote letters after letters, begging Stephanie for a return visit from her, and Stephanie who was usually overcome with guilt and anger about their separation would react.

It hasn't been proven that he actually pursued Stephanie Brooks, in the spring and summer of 1969 he got very close. He was on a hitchhike to California and managed to locate the exact location of her office from the place she worked. Evidently, she was hanging around until she was done with work, he strolled close behind her and, in the most unprofessional way he could have done it the he reached to her and placed his hand over her shoulder. Astonished, she then looked around and realized the source of the unjustified intrusion into the privacy of her was the name of Ted Bundy.

Despite Bundy's strange method of communication, Stephanie was fairly welcoming to him, and admitted a small amount of satisfaction to be seeing him. However, if Ted believed that just bringing her again face-to-face will magically restore their bond back to its former time, Ted was sadly mistaken. Following their short conversation, Bundy only managed to verify Stephanie's opinion she chosen the right path. To this point in his career, Ted Bundy was going absolutely nowhere. He'd dropped out of college and as it was a matter of time that he drifted off to his home in California He appeared to being literally "drifting" through life.

Chapter 9: Ted Becomes Determined

People think that we can have an opportunity to do something different in our lives the chance to begin with a fresh start, learn from our mistakes and then go with our own feet once more. Ted Bundy's next act took place following Stephanie's third refusal to accept his invitations. He was now motivated by a lingering sense of retribution and also his own ego-driven desire to be a success. Ted may not have fully grasped the dangers in his soul. He only knew that the desire was to chip away the flaws of his previous life and to make himself into a huge achievement that no one will ever want to be a part of again.

This new mental attitude and laser-sighted focus that He was able to return to the University of Washington in the autumn of 1969. Instead of pursuing Chinese the student enrolled in classes on Psychology and he was able to earn fast A's. Then, many of his instructors were fascinated by the student. They would later write their praises to students who were scholarly by way of formal letters of recommendation to at the University of Utah Law School where Ted Bundy planned on attending following the completion of his college degree.

In spite of the academic pressures that Bundy endured in his activities, he also had time for some playing time. He became the regular guest at some of the bars on campus that he would frequent late in the evening. In an establishment known as"the "Sandpiper Tavern" that Bundy was introduced to a woman who was named Elizabeth Kloepfer, who like Stephanie earlier was to become the main central point in Bundy's life. Elizabeth also seemed to play the role of a mentor for Bundy as she was three years older than her, and she was already married and divorced.

It is ironic that she divorced her husband just as she discovered his past criminal record that was he tried to hide from her. Looking back, it's unbelievable that she'd leave the supposed "criminal" for the embrace of Ted Bundy, a man who is perhaps one of the greatest serial killers recognized. Naturally, it was not a role in the future that nobody would have been aware of Ted Bundy of fulfilling at that moment. On the night Elizabeth Kloepfer met Ted Bundy the man seemed to be one with everything as if he held everything in a single string.

They had in the bar. Later, after Ted ordered Elizabeth one of his beers, Elizabeth gave him her number. On the next day, when her euphoria of the previous night had worn off, she'd almost lost track of the conversation of Ted Bundy. It was a surprise for her to expect him to contact her at all, but when he called her, she was ecstatic. According to her memories, it was that he was an attractive young male and was a fantastic speaker, so she was curious to find out more. Many have speculated that it could be because of the intense studies of psychologist Ted that he learned how to significantly enhance his communication skills and develop rapport with other people.

It was evident that the aloof and timid Bundy has gone and been substituted by a charismatic and extremely manipulative Bundy who was able to captivate his victims until death. However, before that was over, the primary victim of his appeals to charm would be Elizabeth Kloepfer. She immediately fell in love with the guy. Ted Bundy, the new and improved Ted Bundy that is--seemed to be a confident and successful person and Elizabeth attracted to his confidence-filled light the way a moth is drawn towards a flame.

In fact, she started talking about marriage since the beginning of their romance. It turned out to be Ted that was seen as being the most unpopular partner who was who was a bit shrewd his way, and repeatedly rejected his attempts to woo Elizabeth and informed her that a marriage was only possible after Ted had finished his education and began an occupation. Elizabeth herself agreed with Ted's argument but was also willing to be patient and wait. Elizabeth was ready to use her personal savings account to fund Ted's schooling if needed to be.

Ted continued to work in part-time jobs to help pay the cost of his schooling, however he ran into financial difficulties. When he was in a state of desperation that Elizabeth always appeared and pull out her wallet to assist him. Sometimes, she was worried that Bundy used her to get money, but Bundy was so gracious and thoughtful of her she quickly put these worries aside. In addition, Ted soon landed a higher-paying job that could allow him to pay his ways. In the midst of all opportunities to gain one, Ted landed a salaried job for Seattle Crisis Clinic. Seattle Crisis Clinic answering phones for the suicide hotline.

The work that he did enhance Ted's study in Psychology certainly however, after the infamous crime he was later found accused of, it is strange to have the cold, determined killer in charge of an anonymous suicide hotline! One of his colleagues in the Crisis Clinic, and a later writer of one of the works on Ted Bundy, Ann Rule was later to say, "Ted Bundy took lives" however "he also saved lives." It appears that he may have been a life-long paradox.

In his time in the Crisis Clinic his relationship with Elizabeth Kloepfer seemed to exist in a bizarre condition of indeterminacy also. He regularly spoke to Ann Rule about Stephanie and how he was torn with her over his current girlfriend Elizabeth. According to Ann the former boyfriend was devastated over being able to keep Elizabeth all the way while he was still in love with Stephanie more than any other person. When she learned the background of the tale and the fact that Stephanie broke off their marriage four years before, Ann thought Ted's continued attraction was perhaps a bit obsessional, but there was no sign that alarms rang.

The woman simply saw him as a very intelligent, beautiful young man that wanted to put all his choices open. That is, he would like to enjoy his cake and eat it too if that were even likely. As he shared with a Crisis Clinic coworker, he thought that the largest gap between himself as well as Stephanie is the physical separation as a whole and he was convinced that if he simply make the journey to Washington to California and get her back, he'd be able to bring her back. To overcome this gap the Bundy's goal upon graduating to enroll in an Law School in or around the San Francisco area where Stephanie lived.

Like clockwork, Ted's graduation ceremony from the University of Utah went as was scheduled for July of 1972.

However, Law School would have to be delayed for a few more months because Ted was involved in other pursuits. He was, for instance, hired to assist in the campaign to re-elect the Governor at the time of Washington state Dan Evans. Bundy who was always an uncompromising conservative Republican was ecstatic to collaborate with such a well-known campaign for his Republican party. The opponent of Governor Evans was known as Albert Rosellini. Rosellini was the Governor of his time along with the Evans administration was deeply concerned about the possibility of him stealing the elections.

They were looking to listen at the ground to discover the things their adversaries were engaged in and, in some manner they determined they thought Ted Bundy was just the person to watch their rival!

It was a shady investigation into political intrigue at the top of its game. On the heels of Nixon's criminal dealings with Watergate, Ted Bundy was fitted with a wire to document the Democrat running for Governor's office's every decision. The tapes were later given to Dan Evan's campaign team so that they could review it for things they could later utilize against Rosellini in the course of campaigning.

The idea was similar as stealing another soccer team's rules of play, but this tactic proved to be effective as Governor Evans was able to win re-election. Bundy was later rewarded handsomely by being appointed to an organization called the "City of Seattle's Crime Prevention Advisory Commission". Ted was still planning to attend Law School, but he wanted to advance through into the top ranks on the Advisory Commission, with the extremely optimistic goal that he would be promoted to Director of the Board.

However, to his utter dismay and dismay, his position at the Advisory Commission seemed to be at a standstill and as things weren't progressing at a pace that was satisfactory for his needs, he finally removed himself from the position in the month of January 1973.

It is interesting to note that Ted Bundy's idol, Republican President Richard Nixon and the president of both the Party and the administration Bundy would like to be in, would also be required to step down one year after.

In 1973, Ted appeared to have found his political life to have been a dead end for him. He was seeking ways to get out of the perpetually confusing maze of his existence.

While he was completing undergrad with an impressive GPA, Bundy had managed to misplace with his LSAT score (LSAT refers to the Law School Admittance Test) and was consequently rejected for admission at a number of Law Schools that tend to put more emphasis on test scores for admission rather than GPA's.

With a flood of recommendation letters, and even a positive news from Governor Evans from Washington, Ted was finally admitted to Law School at the University of Utah Law School.

The man was happy to admitted, however his the admission here put a stop to his plan to get together with Stephanie once more in California. His partner Elizabeth is on the other side with relatives already who resided in Utah, was ecstatic at the prospect of their promising future expanding into

Utah. But if only she had known how dark the future could be in the near future.

Chapter 10: Ted Bundy Sets his Plan in Motion

Whatever his success was, in the end Ted Bundy was still very uncertain, and one of the ways that he was able to cope with his insecurity was by having the backup strategy. Whatever the eventuality could be, he was required to have a variety of contingency plans carefully implemented to be prepared in the event that his plans went to pieces. A large part of his insecurity doubt stemmed from his difficult early years, and it's been suggested that the emotions grew exponentially after Stephanie was first able to break his relationship in the year 1968. It was this that triggered the breakup.

If Stephanie Brooks left Bundy high and dry in the year '68, she was completely devastated, an empty body of a person, and with no one to rely to for support. He was determined that he would never be the same again. Whatever the circumstance could have been - whether it was a relationship with a girl or job, or alternative opportunity, he was certain that he always had an escape strategy in place. He sat for the remaining of his life debating, bargaining, as well as wheeling and dealing in the same way. Every decision he took it was accompanied by a countervailing background shadow there within the shadows.

It was the case that while he was received by the University of Utah Law School however, he also had an offer from the University of Puget Sound Law School located in Washington in the background to make sure he was ready. This was very beneficial to him as within a short time prior to the anticipated starting time at University of Utah Law

School He was able to be hired as an advisor for Ross Davis the then chairman of the Washington State Republican Party. The position was not just highly regarded but was also very lucrative in the course of time.

Bundy was set to earn an annual salary of $1000 which was an adequate amount for him in 1973. (About $6500 today, based on current standard.). Ted was never able to get this kind of steady income before at any point in his career and could not decline it. That's why it was that he devised a totally false story to present to the admissions committee at the University of Utah Law. The admissions board was informed that he was involved in an automobile accident, and because of his degenerative condition, he would not be able to continue attending in the near in the near future.

Even as the plan was being crafted, the man was discussing plans about taking night classes in the University of Puget Sound Law School in the autumn semester of 1973. It was due to the connections he had with Washington State's Republicans that Bundy was able to work on an alternative plan which had put off in his thoughts; the rekindling of an affair that he had with Stephanie Brooks. Ted was sent by the Washington Republican Party to Sacramento, California as part of his job as a member of Washington State's Washington Republican Party, and as soon as his plane arrived on the runway in California Ted didn't waste time in reaching out to his old lover.

Then, when Stephanie was finally able to get together with Ted Bundy, she could not have been more awed and amazed with how much Ted Bundy had come.

After dinner, the pair were both impressed. the same evening, she was impressed by his style of speaking and his confidence. Also, she was impressed with the way He was able to do an excellent job for the Republicans and was also taking law classes every week three times with UPS Law. Stephanie was fascinated by this transformation, and became curious about re-examining her possibilities in a relationship with Ted Bundy.

Ted's scheme of getting Stephanie back in his life was a an unstoppable successful. Stephanie came over to see Ted later in the autumn, and was able to join Ted for dinner at his newly appointed boss's residence, in which he was able to introduce her to his wife and with no apparent objection from Stephanie or anyone else. This was all happening without his second lover

Elizabeth having any knowledge concerning the whole thing. However, Ted would end his engagement as soon as he could for him.

With the cold, calculated moves of a chess player who was a mental player in 1973, when the season came towards a close, Ted took every step in his capabilities to ensure that Stephanie be in love to him again. When Stephanie was in his grip, and was openly discussing the couple's marriage and life, Ted purposefully grew distant. He stopped being interested and would often ignore her for long periods of moment. What happened was Stephanie returning to California at the beginning of January 1974, a very upset and confused young lady. The young woman was unsure of what was doing wrong that caused this kind of change to been able to get over Ted.

The truth is, she did not do anything wrong and had performed her job perfectly, because there was a moment within the depths of Bundy's twisted mind, his determination to have Stephanie back was transformed into a stronger desire to retaliate. He wanted to make her feel how he felt, when she left him, and so through a highly intricate, carefully orchestrated plot, the he won her heart so that he could brutally throw her away, just like he thought she had been to his.

Stephanie was stunned She couldn't imagine what had transpired to her. She was devastated that she decided to start consulting a psychotherapist in order for help with her devastated feelings. In all the pain, she never received even a single message from Ted. Each correspondence or inquiries she made to him did not receive a response. It wasn't until months of silence after which she was able to get him on the phone.

Once Ted was picked up, she started to ask him how he can behave so rudely and smug in cutting her off without a reason. Ted promptly responded, "Stephanie, I have no idea what you mean." Then he hung on the line, effortlessly end all ties to the woman he so obviously longed for over the years. It was the last time Stephanie Brooks would here from Ted Bundy, until his image would be featured on the evening news with reasons that nobody could have thought of.

Chapter 11: A Killer on the Move

It was an odd coincidence in the air throughout 1974, relating to something that seemed to be a harmless situations. In 1974, Ted Bundy had begun to eliminate classes in the University of Puget Sound Law School. It was odd that every day he cut the class, the girls would go missing. Evidently, nobody would think to the fact that Ted Bundy was cutting class to abduct, kill, and abuse young women across the western shores in the United States.

It will take a lot of time in addition to many deaths to comprehend the reason why this neat and well-educated young man could be able to commit a crime like this. The death toll of his murders would grow nevertheless. While it is not possible to established beyond a shadow of doubt as to who the first victim could have been based on the confessions he made and the evidence that was gathered following the incident--the initial known victim is an 18 year old University of Washington student named Karen Sparks.

The girl was asleep and totally unaware that an UPS Law School student named Ted Bundy was searching for an entry point into the apartment. Karen's home was located situated on the bottom floor and the only means of entry to and out was via an outside door. Ted was able to sneak into her home, as she lay asleep, the rod was removed from the bed's frame. Then he used the rod as a weapon to kill her, pounding her several times in the head by using the rod.

It's not known how she managed to awake and see the severity of her injuries, but she was bound to suffer irreparable brain injury shortly after. To make his crime more horrific, following the incident Bundy attacked the girl's head with a rod, he then used the rod made of metal and put it repeatedly into her vagina, causing serious internal damage. The woman was hospitalized in a coma, for ten days following the incident as well as being completely disabled for the remainder all of her existence.

The police at first were confused by the absurdity of the act. The victim was not really "raped" in the traditional way (as horrifying as it may be) via direct encounter with the person who committed it however, rather, he was brutally attacked by a bed rod, in the form called "simulated rape", they thought the victim was a person extremely angry, and had a rage that he was expressing on various females. In retrospect, it's extremely telling that it was just following his cruel and calculated break-up with Stephanie when he penned this horrific crime.

The twisted Bundy's mind was he putting the rage the man still held towards Stephanie and innocent victims? The police didn't take long to analyze the crime, prior to when Bundy struck again. The early hours on February 1st, Bundy broke into a second basement apartment to kidnap and attack Lynda Ann Healy. He was also one of the University of Washington student, and was a popular one, at that. Healy was a popular radio presenter in a well-known broadcast titled "Northwest Ski Reports" in the course of which she would provide regular report on traffic and weather covering the entire Washington region.

Her night out was with her friends that night prior to attending a local pub

However, her roommates came to check on her the next morning, she disappeared without trace. There was not a trace of an incident or even a snooze. Her bed was carefully tucked away. Because everything was neat and neat, the guests automatically believed that she had gone to her early morning shift on the radio station, without they even realizing they were missing something. When her boss at the station began to ring their roommates' home phones, they realized that there was something wrong.

They were still not sure what happened to their dear friend. However, the moment police officers arrived and examined her at her, pulling it back covered in a cover, they were astonished by what they found. There were deep, red bloodstains on her pillows. It was evident that Healy was a victim of attack and taken away. They went back to her room and found her night gown, which she could be wearing at the time of the attack occurred since the dress was also covered.

It was oddly evident that following the slamming of Healy to the point of unconsciousness, the attacker was able to take her dress off in a meticulous manner and then hang her bloody garment out of sight, within the closet. After noticing the fact that Healy's blue jeans, white blouse, as well as her favourite booties were not there The perpetrator could be dressed with this outfit before dragging the victim away.

Healy was a regular on the radio station, which was well-known to thousands of local listeners however, once Bundy was in her way the station would not be ever heard of for the rest of her life. When the

Seattle station shut off, Bundy would strike out slightly further away from the capital of the state, in the city of Olympia. The second time, a youthful female student was reported in the wrong place at Evergreen State College which was located just south of Olympia in the proper. The girl's name was Donna Gail Manson, similar to the other victim who disappeared when she was getting ready to go out on a major night at the college campus she was attending with her fellow students.

The plan was to be a part of a group of friends at a renowned jazz club, but she never showed at the venue. Her disappearance was completely unnoticed on the 12th of March, 1974. While the evidence in this case was next to nothing, the resemblances with the earlier assaults and disappearances were striking and sufficient for authorities to conclude that they could have an infamous serial killer on their feet. On April 17 just as if it was a confirmation it was the same story repeated it again, and this time, the events took place further away from Seattle around 120 miles.

This was an obvious evidence that they found a serial killer in their side, but in fact a serial killer who was in motion. The next victim was a girl called Susan Elaine Rancourt she was just starting her freshman year as a student at Central Washington State College but she already became a major attraction on the campus. Her beauty was breathtaking with bright blue eyes that were adorned with lengthy blonde locks as well as an athletic, perfect build that made her male classmates jumping over each other to be able to spend time with her.

While these exterior aesthetics are important, Susan also had a character that was just as beautiful as her physical appearance. She was extremely intelligent, and possessed a love of research, and a desire to focus her studies in biology, and her job in medical research. However, that wasn't enough until she was fortunate enough to run into Ted Bundy. Her room was empty. in the dorm room to wash some clothes into the washer shared by all dormitories after which she went to an advisory meeting on campus with the intention of returning for drying her clothing.

The problem was that Susan was never back to dry her clothes to dry. Always responsible, and never an innocent girl who takes her clothes off without reason and never return, police from the college was immediately called in to inquire about the incident. Although they found

144

nothing to indicate what occurred to Susan but they did uncover unsettling stories from people who were witnesses to the man who was regarded as being a little odd. The man was carrying a book around his wrist and asked some females to help carry his books.

His manner of conduct was charming and polite, however the people who saw him might refer to it as the sixth sense, or something else, but these women were able to see past his smile and feel that something was not right, such as they had stepped through a trap likely to be released. Somebody was instructing them to stop whatever they were doing, and to get clear of Ted Bundy as fast as they could. But they weren't done making quite interesting observations regarding Bundy.

One girl he persuaded to carry books back to his vehicle recalls being with him as he walked up the hill to an antique Volkswagen Beatle parked out of people's sight. The moment they saw the car, she was immediately aware that the passenger's seat was not present in the car and, when she saw this, remembers her "hairs on her neck" were raised and she dropped the books onto top of the vehicle and fled the car with the confidence that her life would be on the situation. It didn't seem like it, but it likely happened.

Chapter 12: The Killer Gets Cornered

Many have referred to Ted Bundy as being a real-life poster child for sociopaths. There is nothing more evidence to this notion as the fact that when Bundy was kidnapping and violently killing girls from all over Washington state while working for an organization called the Washington State Department of Emergency Services (DES)--helping to oversee the search for those girls he took away--in the daytime. While it was as outrageously outrageous and unethical as this would seem to anyone else, Bundy was able to take his victims' lives and make it appear as if he was an integral part of the team to find their bodies!

It appears that he fits the socially ill-advised definition He was able to effectively compartmentalize and isolate the terrible actions he committed while continuing in his regular 9-5 existence in the same way as if he did not worry about the world. There would be many more victims and, as corpses piled up, Bundy seemed to think that he was the best of them everything, and that nothing could affect his. Then, the Teflon Don was set to collapse. Ted Bundy was getting just slightly too confident, and relaxed with his targeting of his targets.

The first crack in his dark armor was around mid-July 1974 in the State Park in Washington. When Bundy was process of attempting to attract an innocent woman identified as Janice Ott to his car in the disguise of wanting assistance "help", nearby park patrons over heard Bundy introduce himself as "Ted". The man was reported to be quite "good looking" and he had on an unisex white short-sleeved top with white shorts and tennis shoes that were white. The officers also noticed that he was wearing what looked as a new cast in his right arm, as though it was a recent injury.

The incident was obviously an important point of reference, considering that many others had also reported seeing the sighting of a man wearing a sling, or a cast on his arm at the same moment that the other girls disappeared too. For Janice it was the same. She too seemed to be mysteriously missing following this incident and, due to recklessness of the culprits, those who were who were present at the scene had an initial name as well as a person to link to the disappearance. They were aware that the women weren't combusting at will They knew that the attractive young man wearing the white pants, shirt and a cast been involved in this.

Also, there were accounts of the same person being seen in an interesting vehicle, the bronze Volkswagen Beetle. When the details of Ted began to pile up and the sketches of a sketch artist from police identified as Ben Smith was able to draw an impressive sketch of the suspect based on the eyewitness account. For Ted Bundy's former colleague in the Crisis Center, Ann Rule the sketch was convincing enough that she believed that her kind courteous, kind, and good character former coworker was indeed an actual "Ted" that they were searching for.

Ann initially tried to deny the idea but then argued that she'd known numerous Teds throughout her lifetime However, in conjunction with the original, as well as other descriptive information, the resemblances were far too compelling for her to overlook. One thing she was

150

unsure of if it matched exactly with the descriptions of the eccentric "Ted" who lured women to death was that the "Ted" had a Volkswagen Beetle and Ted Bundy Ted Bundy she knew never ever owned a vehicle. Hopeful that this little bit of info could help exonerate her friend who was formerly in his place in Crisis Center, Ann contacted the Seattle's most experienced homicide detectives, a guy identified as Dick Reed.

She telephoned Reed to him and explained, "I have a good acquaintance named Ted He's around 27 years old according to the description. I'm not even sure if that he owns a car, as I used to offer rides to him. I'm trying to figure out whether he's got a car in the present. Do you have the ability to do this?" The seasoned detective was then able to assure her that it was possible to conduct an anonymous search in order to discover. Ann accepted the offer and, after revealing Bund's identity Detective Bund said that it would be back to her regarding the findings.

There was barely a minute in the time until the detective Reed phoned her back and shared his findings "Theodore Robert Bundy. 4123 12th Avenue N.B. Do you think that an '68 bronze Volkswagen Bug (Beetle)?" The result was such that they were a perfect match for the murderer, Ann actually thought the detective was making fun of her. However, she required confirmation another time, "Ann, I'm serious. The suspect is currently at the address and drives the bronze Bug." Through Ann's persistence, despite her suspicions and inability to interfere with a friend's personality, the wall was closing in upon Ted Bundy.

Detective Reed quickly obtained the Ted Bundy's driver's licence at the Bureau of Motor Vehicles and included it in the pile of evidence that was gathered by a variety of suspects. It was not clear if there was anything connected to his involvement in the crime however the fact that Ted Bundy shared so many common traits with the murderer was sufficient to not be denied. However, the only factor that Ted could not ignore at his disposal was the unprobability factor his professional and clean appearance as the Law School student and politically well-connected mover and shaker inspired others.

The majority of people would glance at Ted's education, work as well as personal background and find nothing more than an upright citizen. but they couldn't imagine anyone in Ted's position committed such crimes. it was just too absurd to grasp. However, reality is more often than fiction. Ted Bundy was indeed their serial killer - hiding out of sight, relying on the sanity of his carefully constructed "character" to protect him.

It all would unravel for him on the 16th August of 1975. It was around halfway through 2 in the morning, a alert police officer dubbed Bob Hayward parked just outside of his residence was able to see an old, battered Volkswagen Beetle slowly pass by. He knew the neighborhood inside and out and knew every car that were passing through. The man had never encountered such a vehicle before in his lifetime. With his interest piqued and his curiosity piqued, he switched on his spotlight brightly to get at the license plate on the car.

The driver who was paranoid inside was not taking it in, however and, as soon as he noticed a spotlight from the police hitting his car and he turned his lights completely off and drove away from the police. The officer wasn't able to find the chance to remove the license number, however at this point, it wasn't a problem because this maniac was rushing through the streets of a neighborhood with a high velocity, and for what? obviously he needed to chase the driver. Bundy led him down an insane, winding route when he raced through traffic lights and red light warnings with reckless abandon.

The police cruiser was easily outsmarted by it Volkswagen Beetle however, and was on its trail as Bundy evidently deciding the VW Bug was no match stopped at a station. With no apprehension or fear at all following the adrenalin-inducing chase Bundy was able to get from his vehicle. Then, in a sort like "Aw Schuck's" moment that appeared to be totally insensitive given the circumstances of the speed chase, Ted Bundy grinned at the policeman and said "Well--I guess I'm lost."

But Bundy as the master of manipulation has to be aware that such an absurd excuse was not going to bring any use in the circumstance that he was in. Then officer Bob Hayward with his service revolver pointed towards Bundy's head was not having any of it. He sped at him "You had two stop signs! Do you have your registration and license?" Ted Bundy still enjoying himself gave his license to Hayward. When Hayward examined it, Hayward demanded "Just what are you doing out here at this time of the morning?"

Quick with his prefabricated answer, Bundy offered, "I was at the Towering

Inferno at the Redwood Drive-in, and became lost in this subdivision." The first thing that came to mind breaking through Bundy's story was the knowledge that officer Hayward was patrolling the zone at the start of his shift, and had not taken note of precisely what films were being played; and one of them, the "Towering Inferno" was not among the films. However, Hayward was well and continued to drag Bundy into a conversation, to determine what possible lies he was able to trap the man into.

In the course of this investigation that two additional squad cars rushed on the scene to provide backup However, Bundy did not appear to pose a threat immediately. Hayward was soon to discover a reasons to worry, but with a new angle. While he was talking about the matter with Ted Bundy, Hayward noticed an oddity in the car of Bundy and noticed that the seat of the driver was snatched from the front and was lying prone lying on its back to the back. The police officer then rushed to inquire with Bundy, "Mind if I look in your car?"

Amazingly, in the light of the actual contents in the vehicle Bundy accepted the situation and readily informed the officer "Go right ahead." It would be reasonable to think that after all the training he had received at Law School he would have offered more reluctance in the event of a legal issue or another, but it was evident that he realized that he did not have the option of choosing regarding the situation. When officer Hayward illuminated a flashlight in the car, the first thing he saw was a crowbar lying on the floor at the rear of the driver's seat. the bright light of his flash light illuminated an empty bag that was lying on the floor in the seat of the passenger.

Shining his flashlight and moving around to take a closer look, Hayward saw some things which were concerning in the slightest. Inside the bag were a ski mask an ice pick, a rope, as well as a third the crowbar. One of the first things Hayward's brain was focusing on was burglary, thinking that the man was looking through his area for a way to break into homes. However, the facts were sufficient that Bundy's detention was warranted. He read Bundy the rights he had, scoured Bundy for weapons and then threw Ted Bundy in handcuffs.

Chapter 13: Book 'Em Bundy

While he was not taken to justice in connection to the crime spree Bundy's term Bundy became famous with; Ted Bundy was made to appear before authorities for the first time on the 16th of August on the 16th of August, 1975. Prior to this, the man had never been detained previously in his entire life. That's the reason that he was able release himself so effortlessly in accordance with the law in the form of "personal recognizance". It allows a person to be released from the custody of their choice, if you'd like -- that they'll be back with their own "personal recognizance".

As Ted Bundy was so clean on his track record, they were not able to doubt that he'd not show up for bail and then run out of the town. It was only after Ted Bundy was released and headed back to the house that detective Jerry Thompson who was still active in the investigation of the mysterious "Ted" serial killer case and began putting two and two. The man was not just his first name "Ted" he fit the eyeswitness' description exactly. The man also had the same type of vehicle, the Volkswagen Beetle. Instead of weapons for burglary, the things that were found inside the vehicle were in direct line with the tactics used by the serial murderer.

with crowbars that can be bludgeon ski masks to hide the suspect, and handcuffs that are used to secure. With this knowledge, there was a semblance of a threat of a fugitive killer being released in bail might escape across the nation and escape from their reach once more. However, Ted Bundy proved that he was not going to leave the country. He returned to his residence as if nothing was happening, but allowed himself to be detained again on August 21, for the new charges that were brought against the former gangster. Amazingly, Bundy managed to take the whole thing in his stride. for the most part, he seemed even amazed by what had transpired.

In the event that he was asked to answer questions regarding the objects inside his vehicle He explained each one of them. He claimed he had located the handcuffs in an outside trash container and then put them in his vehicle because he thought they were interesting to look at. As for the mask made of pantyhose? Bundy stated that he had added it to his ski mask for additional padding to protect against elements. Also, of course on the face mask itself the man was certain to say that the masks were, indeed used to accomplish exactly what they were intended to serve: skiing.

What about the garbage bags, crowbars and Ice picks?

Bundy was able to dismiss this questions off as totally absurd and claimed that these were everyday items most people have in their vehicle. While in the custody of police Ted Bundy was coerced into entering into an "permission to search" release form that allowed police to take a quick tour of his home and with Ted Bundy present with them. Because it was merely the permission to search form rather than the equivalent of a "search warrant" the police could not take anything away from Ted Bundy's house even if they find it suspect.

The area in which Bundy lived thoroughly clean one of the few things that seemed unusual was a wheel of a bicycle suspended from a meet hook that had knives hanging from the top of a cutting block. Bundy's sole response to the inquiries about the bizarre display was to smile and inform them that "I like to cook." However, besides some strange arrangements of cutlery, like this one however, there was not any clear proof to directly connect Bundy with the murders. However, regardless of the clean and neat Ted was able to keep his house, after persistent investigations, pursuing every clue they were able to find the police managed to arrest Bundy yet again, this time with charges they were hoping could be successful in bringing him to justice.

The 2nd of October, 1975 Ted Bundy was arrested for the aggravated kidnapping as well as attempted criminal assault. It turned out that in the line-up Ted was compelled to go through only a couple of days prior to, Bundy had been identified by the fish who was able to escape the grasp of this killer and was named Carol DaRonch. Carol. DaRonch had had a frightening encounter back in the month of November 1974, in a nearby shopping center situated in Murray, Utah with a man dressed as police officers. An attractive man dressed in a suitcoat and trousers in green as well as a pair of fresh leather shoes came up to Carol when she was perusing the shelves of a Walden's Bookstore.

The guy informed her that a person claimed that her car was taken over and requested the man to accompany back to her car to inspect the damage. This is where the faux officer, who spoke fast, actually persuaded her to enter the vehicle with him in the pretense that he would transport her to the headquarters for police to file the "official complaint". Once she had gotten inside the vehicle rather than going directly to the police station,, he led her to a remote location away from the prying witnesses and then tried to lock her in handcuffs.

He put a cuff on the wrist of one however, Carol was able to put up a spirited fight and he was unable to put her hands in a cuff, leaving but cuffing her wrist twice. Her hands were still unblocked Carol kept fighting to the death with all her strength. The tenacity she displayed had paid off and she finally managed to exit his car, and then make a getaway at the car. Then she was able to signal a driver who drove her away to the safety of. Carol is the person who Carol who forged the identification for Ted Bundy in the lineup as well as her unwavering assertion the fact that Bundy was the one that had tried to kidnap her, assault her and do God know more, they amassed enough proof for them to request that Bundy appear in court for Carol's kidnapping and assault.

The first arguments in the trial started on February 23 in 1976. Based on the counsel of his lawyer Ted Bundy waved his opportunity to be a juror in the trial instead opting to let the decision be made by a judge on the court. According to people who knew the actor, Ted Bundy was actually quite positive at the beginning of the trial. He was convinced that he would be able to beat the accusations being made against the former. The judge's decision on whether or not he could be convinced in Bundy's favor was largely dependent on one of the witnesses at the forefront of the trial, Carol DaRonch.

At the start of her testimony, it became clear that recalling her terrifying experience of being a victim Bundy was extremely difficult for her. The problem was the icy and uninteresting way of how Bundy was looking at her in the distance, almost unblinking throughout the time she testified. Bundy employed a highly skilled lawyer to cross interrogated the witness and found her making what she believed as a number of factual mistakes during her testimonies. Ted Bundy on the on however, as it was his turn on the witness stand -- was completely relaxed as a contrast, and seemed to have an logical explanation to every question put in his direction.

Ted was able to alter his account in this moment as to the real situation at the time he was stopped by the officer Hayward. Instead of asserting that he was lost, Ted offered an even more convincing explanation of why he hid away from police and said he'd found marijuana in his vehicle and fled so the marijuana could be thrown out of his car prior to when the police stopped him. Ted Bundy was now claiming that it was an attempt to dispose of illegal drugs out of his vehicle, which resulted in the brief pursuit. According to Ted Bundy, it was after the marijuana had been thrown through his windows when he finally complied with authorities and consented to being arrested.

While this explanation has now placed Bundy in the spotlight as being a drug dealer, it was able to distract attention away from more obscure motives that he had for hiding from police at night. Bundy could also negate and defend the defense's assertion that he's a proponent of concealing himself, much as the fake moustache that was worn by the "fake policeman" who attempted to kidnap Carol. The prosecution probed Bundy's background of concealing his face, and reported that Bundy changed his appearance in the course of campaigning in the race for Governor Dan Evans, when he was asked to listen in secret on his opponents.

As Bundy was in the witness stand, the question was direct to him "Have previously donned fake mustaches? Was it not the case that you wore one while you acted as a spy during Dan Evans's campaign? Dan Evans campaign?" However, Bundy stood firm in his defense, saying that he would not have worn any kind of disguise. Following a lengthy series of similar denials and arguments from Bundy his defense, the arguments ended on February 27. The judge who was the presiding judge returned with his decision on March 1, 1976 in 1976.

The judge described the decision as one that was an "agonizing" one, no doubt of feeling any sympathy for the person who suffered of the case, Carol DaRonch however, he equally concerned for the ambitious and intelligent Law student Ted Bundy, whose own trial is probably his closest ever have to work in an actual courtroom. Judges were not happy with his decision. However, having listened to the entire evidence and listened to, he was left with no other alternative but to conclude that Ted Bundy absolutely guilty of the crime of kidnapping aggravated.

Chapter 14: Ted's First Sentence

Ted was the first to be sentenced on the 30th of June in 1976, to an unclear sentence of anywhere from 1 to 15 years in jail. Ted was sentenced to an infraction of second degree and many thought he'd get parole within one year. Of course, this is based solely on the crime the man was originally brought to court over: the attempted kidnap by Carol DaRonch. The police had been a long time suspecting Bundy to be responsible for many other things As investigations took place across a variety of states, including a number of victims and missing women and women, the odds of the charges against Bundy increasing were high.

The biggest of these took place in October 1976 when hairs that were found in the Bundy's older Volkswagen Beetle came back as an exact match for the licensed nurse Caryn Eileen

Campbell. She had been missing since Colorado around the time of her disappearance in January. Caryn had been brutally beaten to death by her attacker using an instrument that was blunt and was beaten so brutally that the tracks of the weapon were forever imprinted onto her skull. The police used the indentations to provide another evidence against Bundy in the belief that they were matched with the crowbar kept in the hands of his.

Based on this fresh information in the case of Ted Bundy they were finally allowed to charge him with the charges of murder. While this was happening, Ted Bundy was being evaluated to determine his worth. Bundy would go through a variety of mental tests and examinations in order in order to discover any indication that the man was likely to be the believed serial killer they believed that he was. Tests for their part were not revealing any peculiarity in Bundy's personality. In the exhaustive tests they ran him through, Ted Bundy could not be identified as having any kind of neurosis or psychosis which could be a reason to believe in his being a killer.

However, Ted continued to proclaim his innocence to anyone who might hear. The most often recipients of the endless declarations was his former associate with the Crisis Center, Ann Rule. Ann. Rule ended up writing many letters to Bundy as he was imprisoned and, despite her assistance in the beginning of the investigation that led to the arrest of Ted and conviction, she ended up being in the awkward circumstance of serving as the condemned man's chief comforter. The vast majority of the letters written between them, Ted did not admit any guilt and he kept justifying his actions.

In a particularly touching letter to Ann (whether out of genuineness or deliberate deceit) John seemed almost on the brink of giving up his hope completely and even ending his own existence. In the eyes of Ann the letter was emotional and could likely reads as suicide notes. The most striking thing was it mentioned that it was the Crisis Center that they had worked for. In reference to the suicidal patients who were able to call the center, he informed her "This will be like the Crisis Clinic however, there would be no answer. The only thing I'm asking for is assistance. I'm just leaving"

Following this poetic declaration, Ted then ended the letter with a reaffirmation of his innocence "Lastly and perhaps most importantly most importantly, I would like to let you be aware that I would like everyone to be aware that I am not guilty. I've never hurt another person in my lifetime. God I trust you." Ann was so shocked by the message that she immediately called Bundy's attorney's office and requested the office send someone to conduct a check on the man. However, Bundy was not dead He was in good health and was able to deny any involvement with the killings.

As the evidence against him increased, it could be difficult for anyone to believe -- no regardless of how sincere the pleas might have been Bundy was not involved with the offenses. Bundy certainly felt the lack of trust, and often expressed this by the disdain was his for his personal attorney. In the midst of waiting for a new trial in Cary Campbell's homicide case, Cary Campbell homicide case he asked for and received the privilege of representing himself as his own lawyer.

Many would argue that it was just Ted Bundy's twisted Narcissism surfacing as evidenced by the fact that he believed that nobody else would be capable of representing him except himself and it was his only option to save himself from being found guilty in the future.

Some of Bundy's former friends were amazed by his determination and ended up trapped between two perceptions and beliefs of him as a man. whether he was motivated by his innocence and rage to be free from his own plight, or was a psychotic narcissist intent on manipulating the system for the benefit of his own goals. In the middle of this bizarre emotional conflict that the people who were close to Ted Bundy best, found themselves in a bind. However, as entrapped in the same way as his beloved ones not even aware the fact that Ted Bundy was on the edge of breaking free completely.

Following his transfer in the Garfield County Jail in Colorado in April for the purpose of defending his charges in connection with the Campbell trial, Bundy requested and received permission to be his own lawyer. Bundy was subsequently scheduled to appear for his initial preliminary hearing on the 7th of June in 1977. Because he was a one of the counsel he had chosen, He was not required to be restrained. This could be the biggest mistake. Since after the judge had declared an adjournment during the hearing and Bundy was granted permission to go to the law library in preparation for his defense, he made use of an unbounded freedom to avoid.

The only thing he had to do was to open an unlocked back door in the library, and then leap to the freedom. It was a double fall and he did be injured on the landing however, despite the discomfort the man made the break successfully. The incident did not go without being noticed however. One woman who was standing in front of the courthouse got the most terrifying experience of her life as she witnessed an individual dressed in a suit, who fell out of a window that was just above her. He was then able to quickly get up and sprint (albeit walking) in the fastest way was possible from the spot. The woman was unable to be able to comprehend the odd sight. Upon returning to the courthouse, she went into the Sheriff's office ask, "Is it normal for people to jump out of windows around here?"

The bewildered comment by a passing motorist which set off alarms signalling which indicated that Ted Bundy had made a escape. Police didn't know what to do if Bundy received any assistance from outside, or if he had even the getaway vehicle that was waiting for him. So roadblocks were set up to catch him if be brave enough to venture out on any of the main roads. In the event that he decided to stay on foot the tracking dogs accompanied by horse-back riders were gathered to search the forests, fields and hills until they came across Bundy. Ted Bundy wasn't going to allow them to escape easily however, as he'd already made a meticulous plan for his escape.

As he was before the judge as his own attorney, he was systematically gazing out the window and looking around at the landscape of the field, for that moment, he decided to carry out his strategy. He even had two sets of clothing to mark the occasion so it was possible to get rid of his attire for court for the purpose of making himself more invisible to criminals. In his normal clothes, his strolled into the city in Aspen, Colorado like everything seemed normal. The reality was that everything was not as normal; Ted was an escaped suspect, a fugitive and a murder suspect.

The shocking announcement of his escape Immediately broadcast on airwaves to inform the concerned Colorado residents to lock the house's locks and keep an eye on their children and stay alert for any unusual actions. After a period of three days and no one was able to locate the person who had escaped then the FBI was brought into the scene. It was an extremely busy summer for the FBI for the purpose of pursuing escapees. Even in the midst of

Bundy's escape from Colorado the bureau had lots of work on their plates after another notorious inmate, Martin King Jr.'s executed of assassin James Earl Ray escaped from the Tennessee prison on the 11th of June.

The prisons in the 1970's appeared to be going through an embarrassing series of incidents, and all authorities wanted to restore trust of the people that convictions for crimes were able to be confined. Bundy however, had walked throughout the city to The Aspen Mountains. Bundy experienced and a seasoned hiker, despite an injury to his ankle, quickly climbed the slope of the mountain, along mountains, before finally upwards, then back to the bottom. As he approached the summit, he set out towards the south, away from Aspen.

At the bottom of the hill towards the south, the man came across a the cabin. It was empty nevertheless, it was filled with valuable things for the wanted criminal, such as food, clothes, as well as a gun. Bundy took these items in and continued on his way towards the south. Bundy was wandering aimlessly by foot. However, that was about to alter when on Sunday, June 12, while walking through the local Golf Course he came upon an Cadillac at the entrance to the parking area. Bundy immediately rushed to get on the road and headed towards the West coast. However, he didn't make it far until he was snatched by the police.

The morning of the Monday early morning hours on June 13 an officer in a patrol vehicle observed the car driving at a random speed, turning around the roads. As if it was drunk driving and a drunk driver, the patrol vehicle immediately stopped behind the vehicle and signaled the vehicle to stop. It wasn't actually the driver who was drunk; It could be Ted Bundy, hungry, exhausted, and beat. It was apparent that he was exhausted due to a lack of sleep that he couldn't even maintain the vehicle in the roadway. It was the first was the first time Ted did not give chase and he didn't have a fight (or flight in the case of) to fight for and was willing to submit with the authority from which the previous time he was able to escape.

The cop at the scene recognized Bundy at the scene which led to an slow-moving end to the manhunt. It is believed that Ted just smiled at the policeman and shook his shoulders in a bid to say "Well--you got me." He then recognized the wanted man with a simple "Hello, Ted."

www.ingramcontent.com/pod-product-compliance
Lightning Source LLC
Chambersburg PA
CBHW071340120626
46546CB00002B/643